JAPANESE BEADWORK

WITH

SONOKO NOZUE

JAPANESE BEADWORK

WITH

SONOKO NOZUE

25
Jewelry Designs
from a
Master Artist

LARK CRAFTS

Asheville

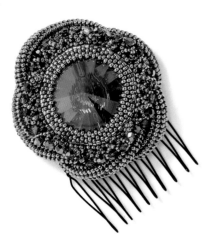

Editor
Nathalie Mornu

Translator
Maki Yamakawa

Technical Editor
Bonnie Brooks

Art Director
Carol Morse Barnao

Illustrator
iwill inc.

Photographer
**Hisamitsu Hayashi,
unless otherwise specified**

Cover Designer
Kathleen Holmes

Editorial Assistance
Abby Haffelt
Larry Shea

Editorial Intern
Virginia Roper

Art Intern
Melissa Morrisey

LARK CRAFTS

An Imprint of Sterling Publishing
387 Park Avenue South
New York, NY 10016

If you have questions or comments about
this book, please visit larkcrafts.com.

Library of Congress Cataloging-in-Publication Data

Nozue, Sonoko, 1945-
  [Mode de beads. English]
Japanese beadwork with Sonoko Nozue : 25 jewelry designs from a master artist / Sonoko Nozue. -- 1st ed.
    p. cm.
  Includes index.
  ISBN 978-1-4547-0278-8 (hardback)
  1. Jewelry making. 2. Beadwork. I. Title.
  TT212.N6913 2012
  739.27--dc23
                                    2011036918

10 9 8 7 6 5 4 3 2

Published by Lark Crafts
An Imprint of Sterling Publishing Co., Inc.
387 Park Avenue South, New York, NY 10016

English-language version © 2012, Lark Crafts, an Imprint of Sterling Publishing Co., Inc.
From *Mode de Beads* by Sonoko Nozue, copyright © 2008 Sonoko Nozue / Wanimagazine Co., LTD.
All rights reserved.
Original Japanese edition published by Wanimagazine Co., LTD.
Photographs / Hisamitsu Hayashi
Illustrations / iwill inc.
Model / Saki Toyoba
Japanese Beadwork with Sonoko Nozue published by arrangement with Wanamagazine Co., LTD. through The English
Agency (Japan) Ltd.

Distributed in Canada by Sterling Publishing,
c/o Canadian Manda Group, 165 Dufferin Street
Toronto, Ontario, Canada M6K 3H6

Distributed in the United Kingdom by GMC Distribution Services,
Castle Place, 166 High Street, Lewes, East Sussex, England BN7 1XU

Distributed in Australia by Capricorn Link (Australia) Pty Ltd.,
P.O. Box 704, Windsor, NSW 2756 Australia

Manufactured in China

ISBN 13: 978-1-4547-0278-8

For information about custom editions, special sales, and premium and corporate purchases, please contact the
Sterling Special Sales Department at 800-805-5489 or specialsales@sterlingpub.com.

Submit requests for information about desk and examination copies available to college and university professors to
academic@larkbooks.com. Our complete policy can be found at www.larkcrafts.com.

CONTENTS

INTRODUCTION

Attend the annual Bead&Button Show and you can't miss Japan's leading bead artist. In a kimono, Sonoko Nozue stands before her table at Meet the Teachers, smiling, posing for pictures, and indicating work she admires by teachers nearby. Wearing all black—a fitted quilted jacket and a contemporary version of the *hakama*, traditional wide trousers—she navigates the conference center halls briskly with translator and assistant in tow, pulling multiple suitcases packed with the gifts and sweets that she showers on her students, friends, and business associates.

For her first workshop at Bead&Button, in 2005, Sonoko taught the dramatic *Sonoko Necklace* featured on the cover of this book. Not surprisingly, 41 students signed up. Three years later she was chosen to instruct the beading Master Class, which was called A Journey with Sonoko Nozue: Beaded Jewelry Inspired by Japanese Kimono Design. Because Sonoko designs and produces her jewelry primarily for lessons, she selects the techniques deliberately, to create designs that are straightforward to make and easy to wear.

She sometimes begins with nothing more in mind than a color palette or specific bead types to use, but other times she waits until she has dreamt up a perfect design. In class, she teaches how to bead precisely, even in the parts of a piece that aren't visible. And while one of her goals is to choose colors carefully with a particular effect in mind, she always urges her students to experiment with different hues.

Sonoko lives in Nagoya, which is between Tokyo and Osaka. She started her beading career at age 48, after finding herself mesmerized by a beaded bag woven with metal beads. Wanting one of her own, she promptly learned loom beading. As she perfected her skills, added techniques to her repertoire, and made a name for herself, she forged close ties with Japanese bead manufacturers—who sometimes give her prototype beads—and she even designed her own brand of beading thread. Sonoko has beaded shawls, scarves, vests, and purses of her own design, principally for exhibition. And of course, there's her jewelry.

Her jewelry has a delicate quality. It's soft and subtle, and completely refined. In these pages you'll find 25 projects with wonderfully evocative names like Dripping of the Moon, Beach at Night, and Sound of Raindrops. (Would you believe Sonoko says she's not good at coming up with titles? Her students usually name the pieces for her!) The projects are made in a variety of stitches, and many are necklaces because Sonoko thinks ropes are the easiest item to wear and the most fun to bead.

Beaders who prefer to pore over illustrations rather than read words will be especially delighted. Using the Japanese approach, these instructions rely more heavily on illustrations than on text. And while the colors in the drawings reflect the ones shown in the project photos, don't forget that Sonoko encourages her students to try out their own favorite colors. So flip through the book. Admire the charming projects and the lovely model wearing them, choose something to make, and learn at the feet of this Japanese master.

— *Nathalie Mornu, editor*

CHAPTER ONE
BASICS

This section includes directions and information regarding the tools, materials, and techniques mentioned throughout the book.

Teaching at the 2007 Bead&Button Show, where I led three six-hour-long classes. My interpreter, Ms. Yamada, is on the left.

Aiko Beads

Aiko beads are cylindrical and produced by the Toho Company specifically for off-loom bead weaving. They have a large hole and are unfailingly consistent in size and shape. Because of this, projects made using Aiko beads will be extremely smooth. Aiko beads are available in one size—an outside diameter of 1.65 mm—and come in approximately 260 colors.

Materials and Tools

Beads

The type of bead you use greatly influences the outcome of any project. The same stitch or pattern can produce a variety of projects if you simply alter the kinds of beads with which you weave. You can create a wide variety of projects if you're familiar with the characteristics of particular beads. The beads described here are all of high quality.

Delicas

Produced by Miyuki, these cylindrical seed beads are perfect for off-loom bead weaving. Delicas are consistent in size, shape, and color, and are available in four sizes: 15° (1.3-mm diameter), 11° (1.6-mm diameter), 10° (2-mm diameter), and 8° (3-mm diameter). Their holes are large for their diameters, making them especially easy to work with in crocheted projects. They come in almost a thousand shades spanning 11 different colors, and are manufactured using nearly 30 different processing methods.

Matsuno Beads

Matsuno beads are glass beads produced exclusively by the Matsuno Company, which was established in 1935. They can sometimes be difficult to find in Japan. Outside of Japan, they're sold under the brand name MGB. Matsuno beads have thick walls and small holes, requiring small needles.

Swarovski Elements

These beautiful crystal beads, manufactured by the Swarovski company of Austria, come in a variety of shapes, sizes, and colors. I often use the 2-mm, 3-mm, and 4-mm bicones and rounds to add brightness and beauty to my work.

Thread

A good choice for off-loom bead weaving is nylon thread. A wax-coated surface makes it easy to string and move beads, and its elasticity makes it easy to tighten. Use thread conditioner as needed.

I worked closely with Kyoto-based Fujix Ltd. to develop my own line of wax-coated beading thread.

Needles

Perhaps one of the most important tools for any beading project is the needle. I recommend John James size 10 and 12 needles. These are very flexible and move with ease through a variety of beads, making the weaving process smooth and simple. Because many projects may require needles of different thickness and length, it's important to have more than one size in your collection.

Symbols

This section explains the symbols identifying different beads and techniques in the illustrations. Note that, depending on the project, the illustrations may represent different types of beads and bead sizes in different ways. Simply refer to this table to confirm the type of bead to use.

A bead that's not outlined in bold indicates it was already woven in a previous step.

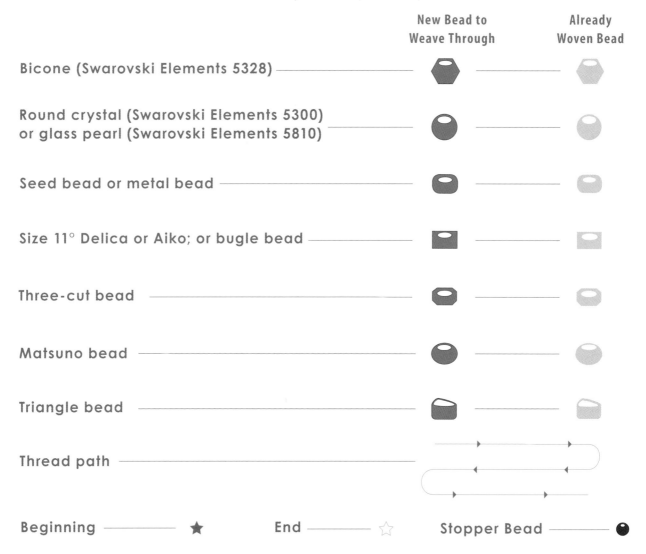

	New Bead to Weave Through	Already Woven Bead
Bicone (Swarovski Elements 5328)		
Round crystal (Swarovski Elements 5300) or glass pearl (Swarovski Elements 5810)		
Seed bead or metal bead		
Size 11° Delica or Aiko; or bugle bead		
Three-cut bead		
Matsuno bead		
Triangle bead		
Thread path		

Beginning ————— ★   End ————— ☆   Stopper Bead ————— ●

- "Swarovski Elements" refers to crystal beads produced by the Swarovski company.

- A charlotte is a type of seed bead made in the Czech Republic. A side cut on the exterior provides subtle light reflections.

- "Metal" refers to metal beads.

- The supply list for each project calls for a larger number of seed beads than is required, so you won't come up short.

- The stopper bead is not included in the supply list given for each project.

- Make sure to use a length of thread with which you can work easily.

- H=height, W=width

14

Techniques

Beginning

A seed bead temporarily attached to the end of the thread is called a stopper bead.

Attach the stopper bead in the following manner: String on 1 size 11° bead and hold it approximately 6 inches (15 cm) from the end. Pass through the bead again and tighten (figure 1).

After you finish weaving your project, remove the stopper bead. You can then use any remaining thread to attach clasps, or weave back into your project to secure the thread before tying off.

figure 1

Adding Threads

Knowing how to add new threads to your project without allowing the others to come loose is important. In my work, I choose simple knots. Here I illustrate a weaver's knot, which is simple yet versatile. (You can use other knots, including the becket bend, the sheet bend, and the square knot, which are easy to find instructions for online.)

1 Hold a short piece of thread in your left hand and another in your right. Cross your threads, placing the right-hand one on top of the left-hand one (figure 2).

figure 2

2 Wind the left-hand thread (the bottom one) twice around the right-hand thread (the top one), as shown in figure 3.

figure 3

3 Using both threads, tie a knot as shown in figure 4, then pull to tighten.

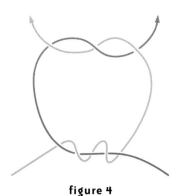

figure 4

Stitches

The numbers in the illustrations show the order of threading.

Zulu Stitch

Make the chevron design by picking up 5 beads and passing back through the fourth bead.

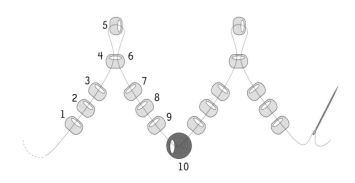

Spiral Rope

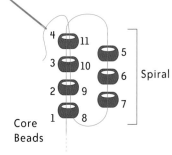

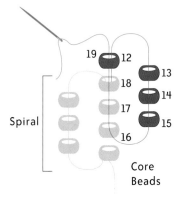

1 Stitch the spiral beads around the core beads. After they're added, the spiral beads should be pushed to the left, in preparation for the next stitch.

2 Add one core bead, then add more spiral beads. Repeat this pattern in order to create a spiral rope.

Chevron Stitch

Create the chevron pattern by weaving the thread through the beads either from top to bottom, or from left to right.

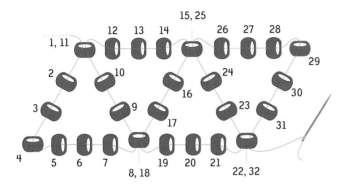

Peyote Stitch

Flat

Circular

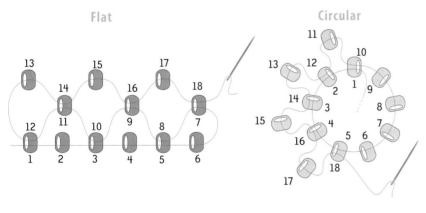

String rows 1 and 2 (beads 1 to 6). Begin row 3 by picking up 1 bead (7); skip 1 bead (6) and pass through the next bead (8). Continue across in this fashion. For each subsequent row, pick up a bead and pass through the next up bead of the previous row.

Begin by making a ring of nine beads. Add additional rounds to the ring by weaving the thread through beads in the previous rows.

***Prism,* 2006**

21 x 9 x 1.5 cm

Faceted crystal rounds, seed beads; chevron stitch

Daisy Chain

All the flowers in a daisy chain pattern adjoin each other. Each flower shares a border of 2 beads with each of its neighbors.

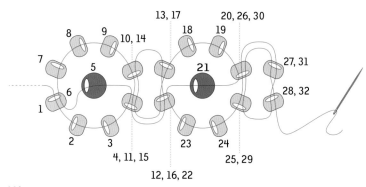

Netting

Weave by passing through beads from the previous row at regular intervals as you pick up new beads.

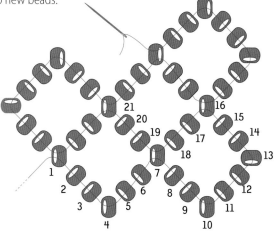

Brick Stitch

1 Create the first row of beads, following the thread path shown in figure 5. (This stitch is also known as ladder stitch because the beads are woven into a shape resembling a ladder.)

2 Weave the subsequent rows by picking up the threads between the beads as you also pick up additional beads, as shown in figure 6.

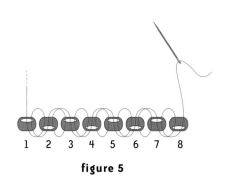

figure 5

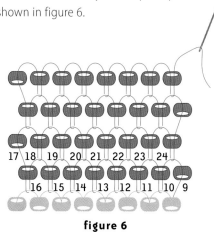

figure 6

Tubular Bead Crochet

1 Begin by stringing all of your beads onto the thread. Then create a slipknot on the crochet hook (figure 7).

figure 7

2 Tighten the slipknot by pulling on the tail (figure 8).

figure 8

3 Move the first bead to the crochet hook (figure 9).

figure 9

4 Move the first bead to the other side of the crochet hook. Then wrap the thread around the hook from front to back. Pull the thread through the slipknot (figure 10).

figure 10

5 You've now chained the first stitch. Move the second bead forward and repeat step 4 to make the second stitch (figure 11).

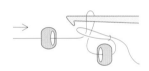

figure 11

6 Repeat steps 3 through 5 until you've made the number of stitches given in the instructions (figure 12).

figure 12

7 Slide your hook through the loop on the left side of the first bead in the first row (figure 13).

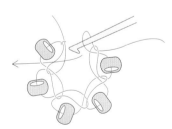

figure 13

8 Turn the first bead over and then bring the first bead of the second row close to the hook (figure 14).

Make sure the hole of the first bead faces up.

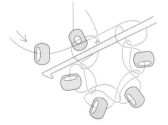

figure 14

9 Using the hook, pull the thread through the loop of the second bead, creating a slip stitch and making it come out on top of the first bead. Repeat steps 7 through 9 until you obtain the desired number of rounds (figure 15).

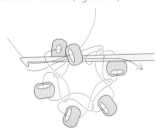

figure 15

CHAPTER TWO

CASUAL

A pop of color adds excitement.

CHEERFUL MIDAFTERNOON

When I found some rare, light-blue Czech beads in an American bead store, I knew I had to make the most of their delicate tone. In creating this design, my first decision was to use Zulu stitch.

SUPPLIES

34 purple Miyuki 10° triangle beads, 2.5 mm

Silver 10° Toho three-cut beads, 16 g

99 bluish Czech lily beads, 5 or 6 mm

Size 15° clear beads, 0.5 g

33 light blue bicones, 5 mm

Two 11° Aikos or Delicas, any color

2 silver cone bead caps

2 silver bead tips

Silver clasp

Gray beading thread

Size 10 or 12 beading needles

Sharp snips

Glue

STITCH

Zulu

FINISHED SIZE

15¾ inches (40 cm) long

1 Using Zulu stitch and following figure 1, make 33 stitches with triangle, three-cut, Czech lily, and size 15° beads.

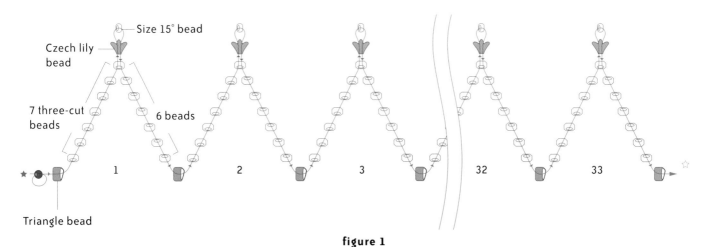

Size 15° bead

Czech lily bead

7 three-cut beads

6 beads

Triangle bead

1   2   3   32   33

figure 1

2 Pass through the first triangle bead picked up in step 1. Pick up three-cut, Czech lily, and size 15° beads, and weave as shown in figure 2.

3 To make picots, first turn down the row woven in step 1. As shown in figure 3, pick up three-cut beads and pass through the triangle beads you picked up in step 1.

4 Pick up new three-cut beads and pass through the top bead of each picot. Refer to figures 4 and 5 (on page 26) for the number of three-cut beads to pick up.

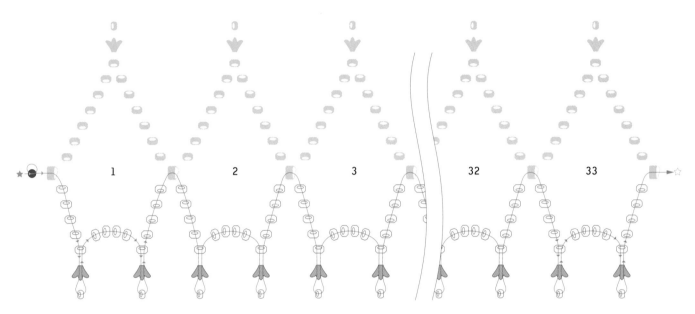

figure 2

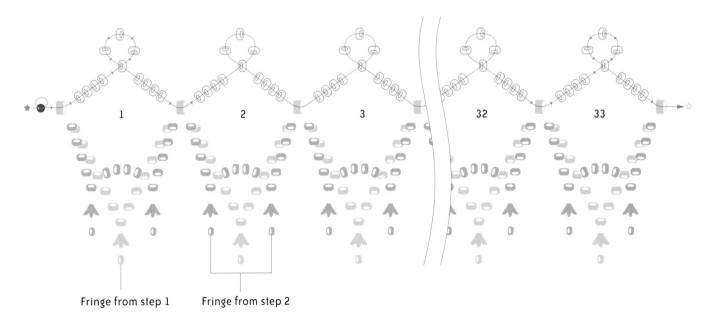

Fringe from step 1   Fringe from step 2

figure 3

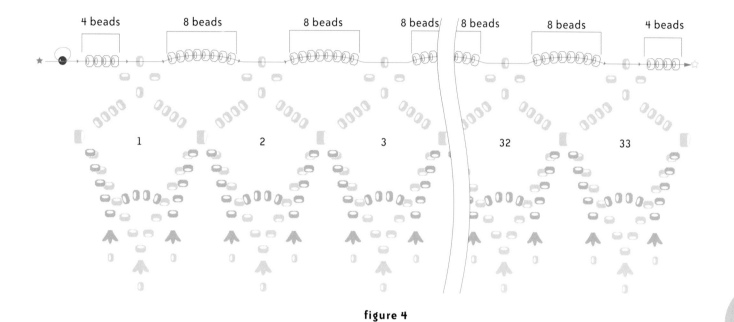

| 4 beads | 8 beads | 8 beads | 8 beads | 8 beads | 8 beads | 4 beads |

1   2   3   32   33

figure 4

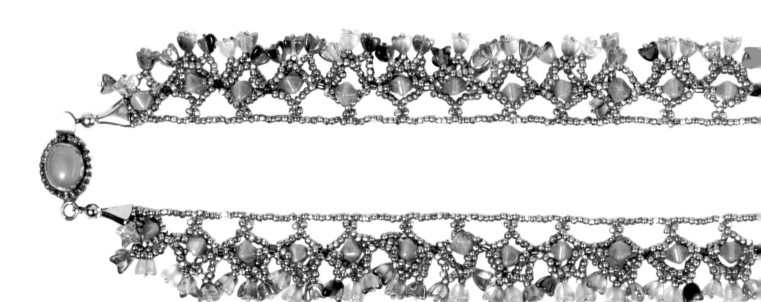

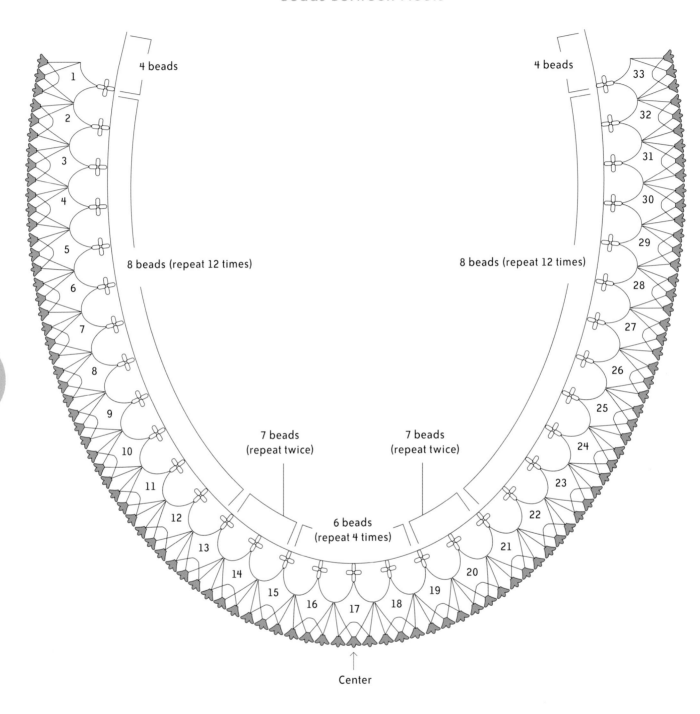

Number of Three-Cut Beads Between Picots

4 beads

8 beads (repeat 12 times)

7 beads (repeat twice)

6 beads (repeat 4 times)

Center

figure 5

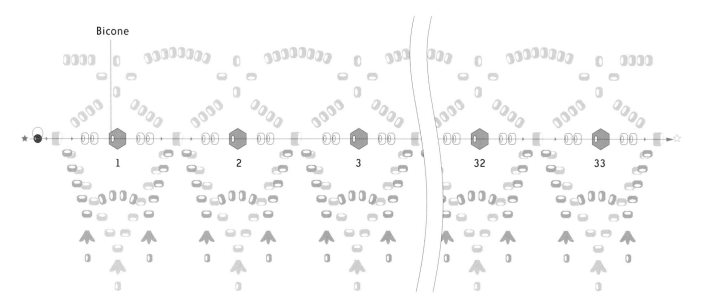

Bicone

1   2   3   32   33

figure 6

5 Pass through the triangle beads and pick up three-cut beads and bicones, as shown in figure 6.

6 On one end of the piece, pass the threads from steps 1 through 5 through a bead cap and then a bead tip. Divide the threads into two equal halves, and pass one half of the threads through an Aiko or Delica. Tie a square knot and glue it. Close the bead tip. Repeat on the other side of the piece.

7 Attach each half of the clasp to a bead tip.

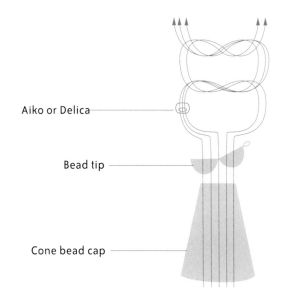

Aiko or Delica

Bead tip

Cone bead cap

figure 7

SHOWER
OF BLOSSOMS

You can create this piece as a necklace at the length given in the instructions, or shorten it and add a clasp to make a striking bracelet. Either way, the combination of sparkling red crystals, gold metal beads, and black thread makes it gorgeous.

1 As shown in figure 1, and starting with thread that's 5 feet (1.5 m) long, string on beads and weave in netting stitch. Whenever your working thread gets short, start a new thread that's the same length as the original one.

2 When you reach your desired length, finish off the threads of both sides by passing back through the beads already woven and making several half-hitch knots.

SUPPLIES

2,182 red crystal bicones, 3 mm
(Swarovski Elements 5328, Light Siam)

1,300 size 15° gold metal beads

Black beading thread

Size 10 or 12 beading needles

Sharp snips

STITCH

Netting

FINISHED SIZE

38¼ inches (97 cm) long

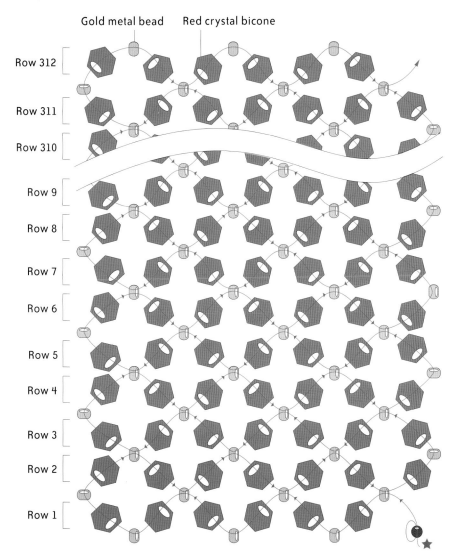

Gold metal bead   Red crystal bicone

Row 312
Row 311
Row 310
Row 9
Row 8
Row 7
Row 6
Row 5
Row 4
Row 3
Row 2
Row 1

figure 1

SUPPLIES

Metallic green 11° Aikos or
Delicas, 15 g

Size 15° metallic green beads, 1.5 g

78 green crystal bicones, 3 mm
(Swarovski Elements 5328, Erinite)

39 green crystal bicones, 4 mm
(Swarovski Elements 5328, Erinite)

3 green crystal flower spacers,
6 mm (Swarovski Elements 3700,
Crystal Vitrail Medium)

1 cameo, 1 x ¹¹/₁₆ inch (2.5 x 1.8 cm)

Silver chain, your choice of length

Gray beading thread

Size 10 or 12 beading needles

Sharp snips

STITCH

Peyote

FINISHED SIZE

Pendant, 8 x 2 inches (20.3 x 5.1 cm)

DRIPPING OF THE MOON

For this pendant, I used peyote stitch to embellish a cameo with seed beads. I treasure this piece because I taught it at the 2007 Bead&Button Show.

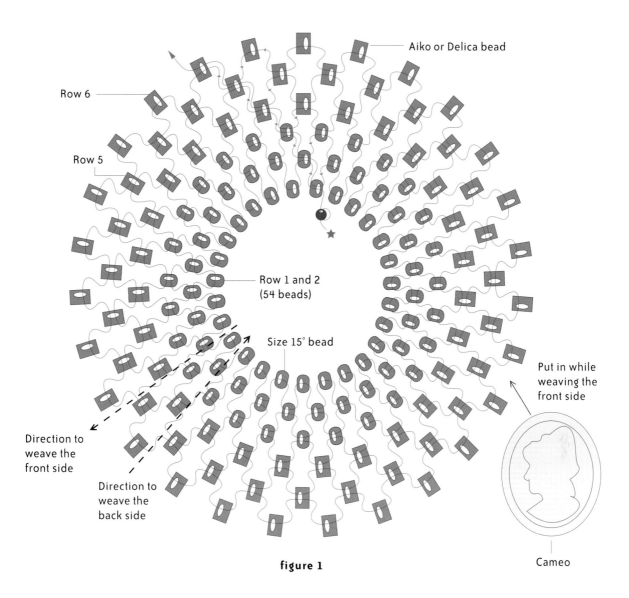

Aiko or Delica bead

Row 6

Row 5

Row 1 and 2
(54 beads)

Size 15° bead

Direction to
weave the
front side

Direction to
weave the
back side

Put in while
weaving the
front side

Cameo

figure 1

► Cameo Bezel

1 Weave 6 rows of circular peyote stitch as shown in figure 1. Then put the cameo into this bezel face down. For the back side, weave 3 rows using Delicas, then 2 rows using 15°s. Cut off the thread.

2 Embellish the fifth and sixth rows on the front side of the cameo with picots, as shown in figure 2. Start with a new thread to embellish each row. Finish off both threads.

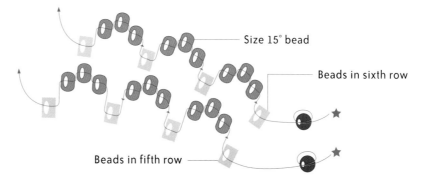

Size 15° bead

Beads in sixth row

Beads in fifth row

figure 2

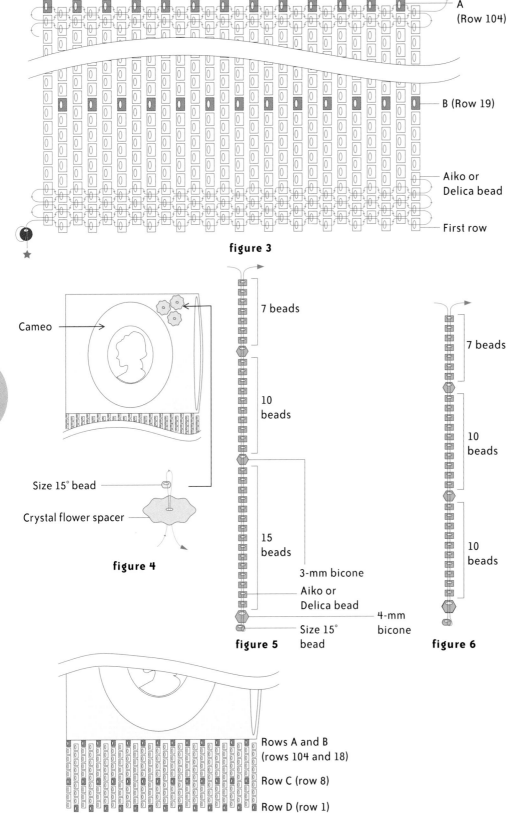

A
(Row 104)

B (Row 19)

Aiko or
Delica bead

First row

figure 3

Cameo

Size 15° bead

Crystal flower spacer

figure 4

7 beads

10
beads

15
beads

3-mm bicone
Aiko or
Delica bead

4-mm
bicone

Size 15°
bead

figure 5

7 beads

10
beads

10
beads

figure 6

Rows A and B
(rows 104 and 18)

Row C (row 8)

Row D (row 1)

figure 7

► Base

3 Weave a piece of flat peyote stitch that's 26 beads wide by 104 rows long, as shown in figure 3. With the remaining thread, go alternately through the A and B beads to zip them and make a tube. (You can proceed to step 4 before making this tube.) When your working thread becomes too short, add a new length of thread 60 inches (1.5 m) long.

4 Using single thread, attach the cameo and the crystal flower spacers to the base, referring to figure 4 for placement.

► Fringe

5 You'll attach 13 strands to each of 4 rows—A, B, C, and D—as follows. Figures 5 and 6 show the bead counts for the two different strands making up the fringe.

For rows A and B, start from the left and alternate adding the strands described in figures 5 and 6, as shown in figure 7. When your working thread gets too short, add a new thread 60 inches (1.5 m) long.

6 For rows C and D, add only strand lengths as shown in figure 6. Weave in and cut the thread off.

7 To finish the pendant, run the silver chain through the top of the tube.

WATERDROPS

This popular class project delights my students with the possibility of putting lots of colors on their wrists. To give this bracelet the proper fit and feel, I prefer to use beads of moderate weight, such as Delicas and size 15° Miyukis.

SUPPLIES

Size 6° purplish khaki beads, 4 g

Purple 11° Delica beads, 4.5 g

Size 15° beads:

   Bronze, 8 g

   Purple, 8 g

   Brown, 8 g

Crystal bicones, 3 mm:

   47 red (Swarovski Elements 5328, Garnet)

   47 matte red (Swarovski Elements 5328, Dark Red Coral)

   47 brown (Swarovski Elements 5328, Smoke Topaz)

Bronze toggle clasp

Gray beading thread

Size 10 or 12 beading needles

Sharp snips

STITCH

Spiral Rope

FINISHED SIZE

7⁷/₈ inches (20 cm) long

▶ **Spiral Rows**

1 Using spiral stitch, pick up 4 size 6° beads for the core and 9 Delicas for the spiral. Pass through the 4 size 6° beads again (figure 1). Before moving on to the next step, move your spiral beads so they're on the left side of your work.

2 Pick up 1 size 6° bead and 9 Delicas. Pass through 4 size 6° beads, as shown in figure 2. Repeat this step until you have 45 spiral rows.

▶ **Fringe**

3 The next step is to add looped fringe at the bottom of the spirals you just made in steps 1 and 2. Pass through 1 size 6° core bead and pick up size 15° beads and a 3-mm bicone for fringes—mix up the colors any way you like—as shown in figure 3. Then pass through the next core bead.

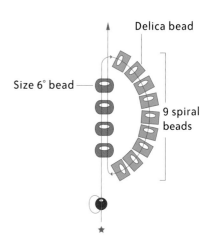

Delica bead
Size 6° bead
9 spiral beads

figure 1

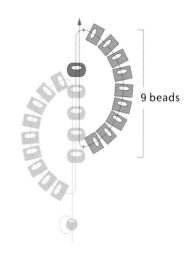

9 beads

figure 2

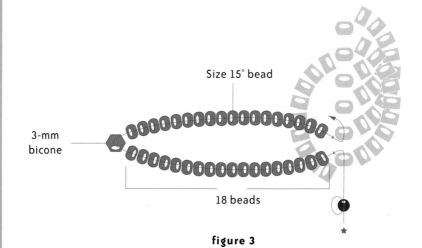

Size 15° bead
3-mm bicone
18 beads

figure 3

4 Using the same method as in step 3, add two more looped fringes at the bottoms of the spirals. With a new thread, pick up size 15° beads and 3-mm bicones in different colors, as shown in figure 4. You'll have three fringes in three colorways, for a total of 141 fringes. (Refer to the photograph on page 33 for possible color combinations.)

▶ **Finish**

5 At each end of the beadwork, pick up size 15° beads, one half of the toggle, and more 15° beads, as shown in figure 5. Weave back into the spiral rope then finish off the threads.

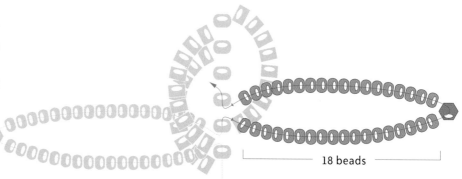

18 beads

figure 4

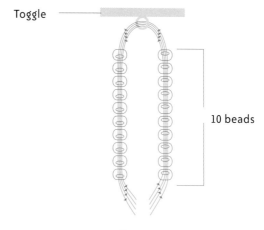

Toggle

10 beads

figure 5

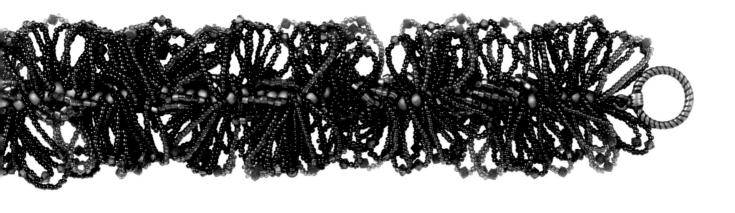

SUNFLOWER

The yellow Venetian-style focal beads that brighten this necklace were handmade by a craftsman in Kichijo-ji, an artsy district of Tokyo. They combine playfully with a variety of seed and bugle beads.

1 Following the thread path in figure 1, string on just the first row by picking up the beads shown. Repeat this pattern 14 times.

2 At the end of the first row, make a loop of size 15° beads that catches one half of the clasp, as shown at the top of the illustration.

Weave the second row as you did the first, then attach the other part of the clasp with another loop of size 15° beads.

3 For the third and fourth rows, pass through the loops of size 15° beads (and clasp halves) again at both ends. When you've finished weaving 4 rows, finish off the threads.

SUPPLIES

Size 15° gold seed beads, 0.7 g

50 gold bugle beads, 3 mm

168 yellow Venetian-style disk-shaped beads, 1 x 3 mm

Size 11° seed beads:

Brown, 5.5 g

Yellow, 5.5 g

Green, 5.5 g

Gold clasp

Gray beading thread

Size 10 or 12 beading needles

Sharp snips

STITCH

Zulu

FINISHED SIZE

22 inches (56 cm) long

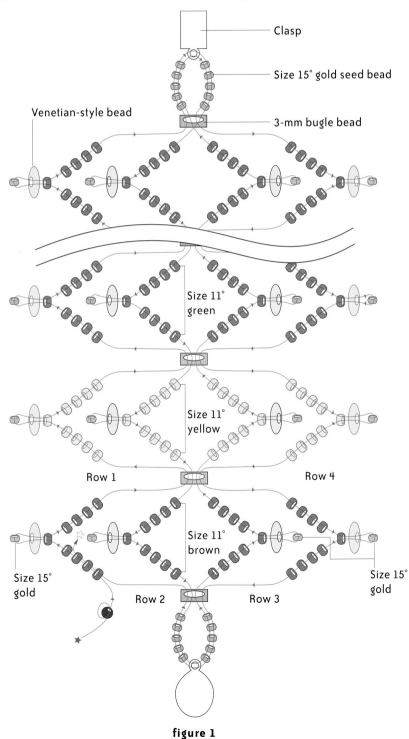

Clasp

Size 15° gold seed bead

3-mm bugle bead

Venetian-style bead

Size 11° green

Size 11° yellow

Size 11° brown

Row 1

Row 2

Row 3

Row 4

Size 15° gold

Size 15° gold

figure 1

CHAPTER 3
FEMININE

These designs embody the happiness of an afternoon spent with friends.

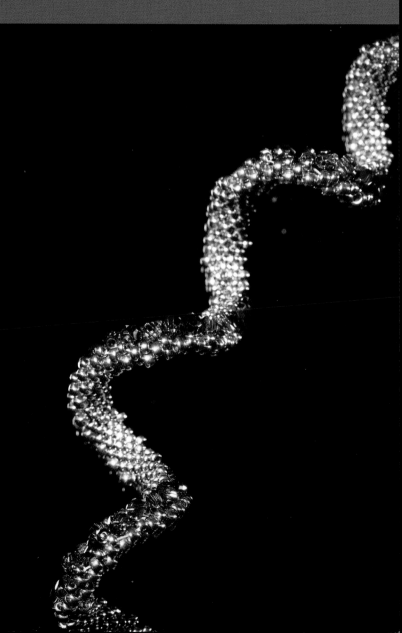

SWEET BREEZE

I taught this netted shawl in a one-day lesson at the Japan Hobby Show in Tokyo. I wanted the piece to be as soft as a fabric, so I took special care with the thread tension—neither too loose nor too tight—and kept my weaving very precise to create uniform stitches.

▶ Shawl

1 Pick up size 11° beads and weave in netting stitch, following figure 1.

SUPPLIES

Size 11° clear beads, 120 g

Size 15° clear beads, 80 g

255 clear AB crystal bicones, 3 mm (Swarovski Elements 5328, Crystal AB)

85 clear AB crystal bicones, 4 mm (Swarovski Elements 5328, Crystal AB)

2 clear AB round rhinestones, 6 mm (Swarovski Elements 1028 SS39, Crystal AB)

White beading thread

Size 10 or 12 beading needles

Sharp snips

STITCHES

Netting

Peyote

FINISHED SIZE

2¾ x 24¾ inches (7 x 62.9 cm), before fringes

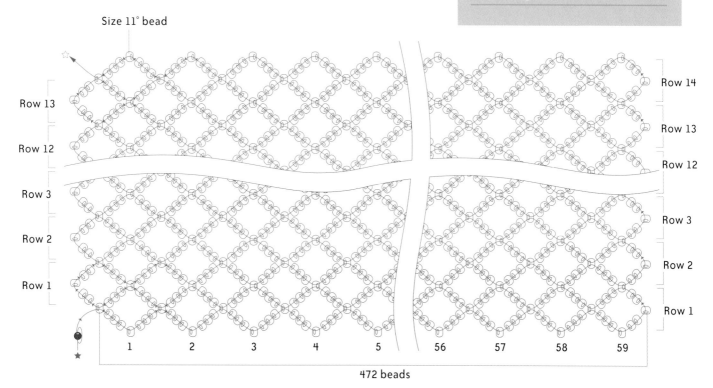

Size 11° bead

Row 13
Row 12
Row 3
Row 2
Row 1

Row 14
Row 13
Row 12
Row 3
Row 2
Row 1

1   2   3   4   5   56   57   58   59

472 beads

figure 1

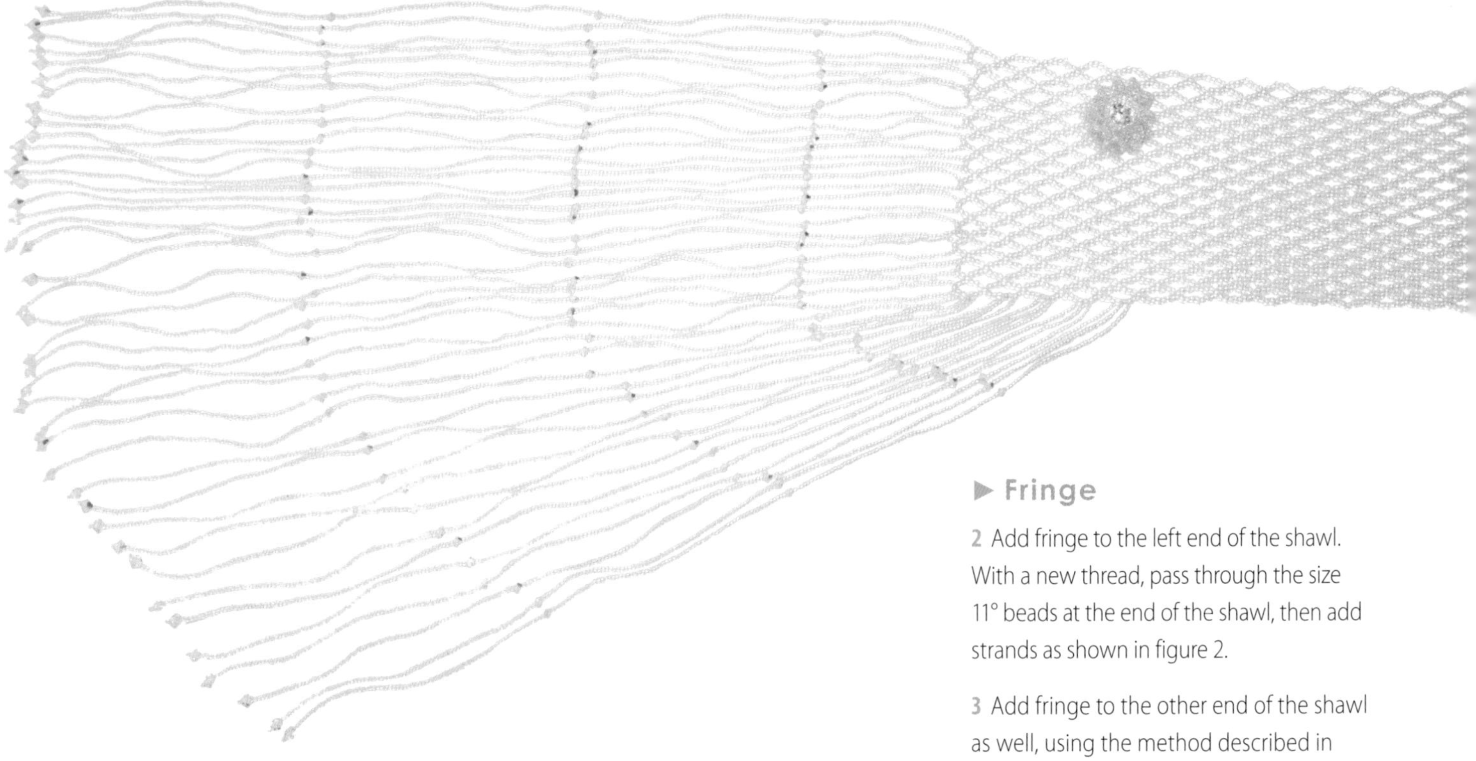

▶ Fringe

2 Add fringe to the left end of the shawl. With a new thread, pass through the size 11° beads at the end of the shawl, then add strands as shown in figure 2.

3 Add fringe to the other end of the shawl as well, using the method described in step 2, but following figure 3.

▶ Decorative Motif

4 To add a decorative motif, first pick up 20 size 15° beads and tie a knot in the thread to form a ring (figure 4).

5 Weave 2 rows in peyote stitch using size 15° beads, then 3 rows using 11°s. After you finish the fifth row, insert a rhinestone face up, then stitch 2 more rows using 15°s (figure 5).

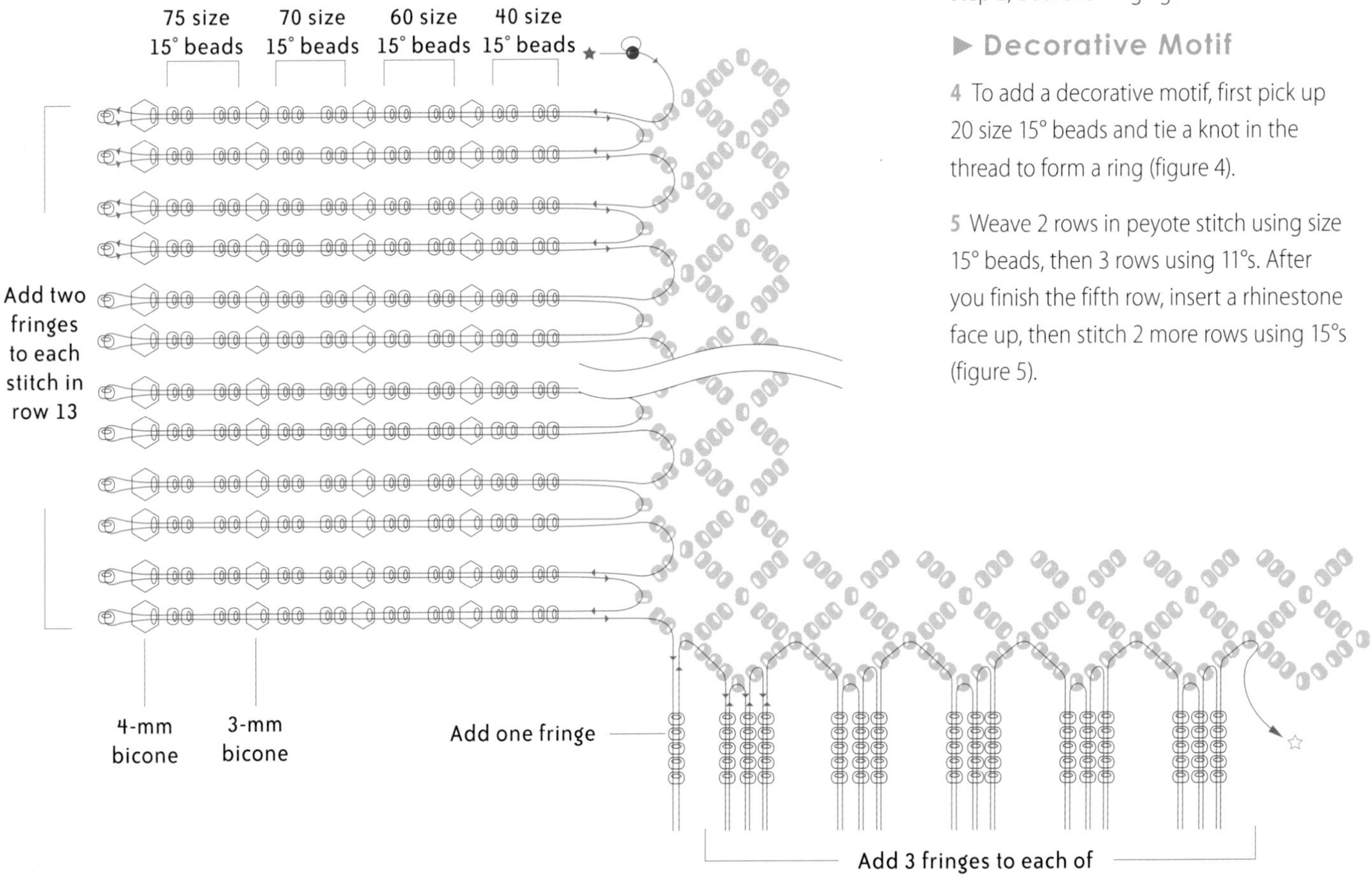

75 size 15° beads   70 size 15° beads   60 size 15° beads   40 size 15° beads

Add two fringes to each stitch in row 13

4-mm bicone   3-mm bicone

Add one fringe

Add 3 fringes to each of the last 5 stitches

figure 2

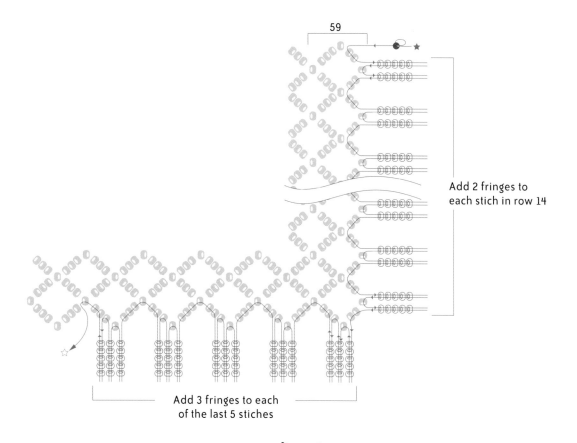

59

Add 2 fringes to
each stich in row 14

Add 3 fringes to each
of the last 5 stiches

figure 3

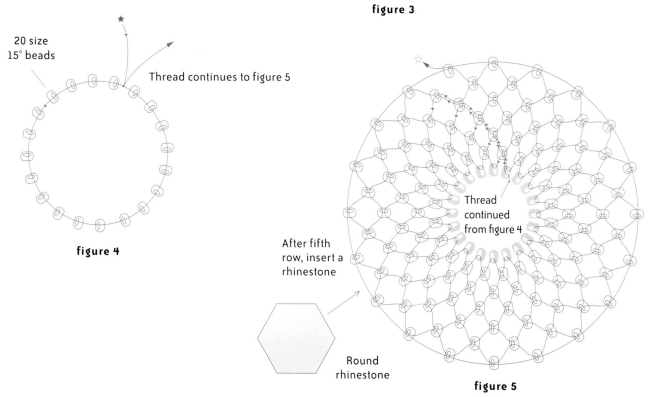

20 size
15° beads

Thread continues to figure 5

figure 4

After fifth
row, insert a
rhinestone

Round
rhinestone

Thread
continued
from figure 4

figure 5

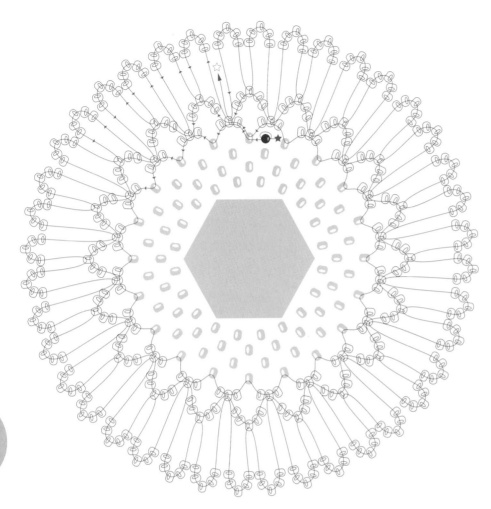

6 Next, embellish the motif. Attach a new thread and come out from a bead in the fourth peyote row, as shown in figure 6. Pick up size 15° beads to serve as picots, adding a total of 3 rows of picots.

7 Repeat steps 4, 5, and 6 to make a second motif.

▶ **Finish**

8 Referring to figure 7 for placement, attach the decorative motifs to the shawl. Weave back in the shawl, then finish off the threads.

figure 6

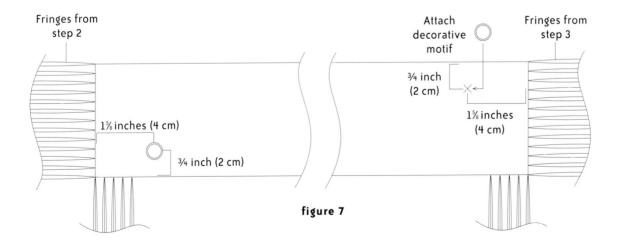

Fringes from step 2

Attach decorative motif

Fringes from step 3

¾ inch (2 cm)

1⅝ inches (4 cm)

1⅝ inches (4 cm)

¾ inch (2 cm)

figure 7

SNOW CRYSTAL

I made this brooch as a gift for a person who has always given me lots of support. When using a single color in a design, you can create a gorgeous look by including shiny crystal beads.

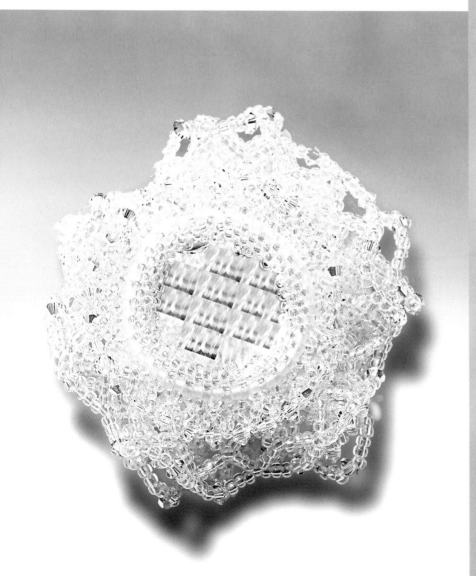

SUPPLIES

Size 15° clear AB beads, 2 g

White 11° Delicas or Aikos, 2 g

Size 11° clear AB beads, 7 g

54 clear AB crystal bicones, 3 mm
(Swarovski Elements 5328, Crystal AB)

1 clear AB faceted sew-on rhinestone,
28 mm (Swarovski Elements 3221,
Crystal AB)

Pin back

White beading thread

Size 10 or 12 beading needles

Sharp snips

STITCHES

Peyote

Netting

FINISHED SIZE

2³⁄₈ inches (6 cm) in diameter

45

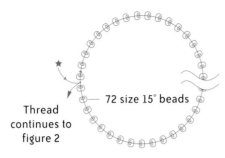

Thread
continues to
figure 2

72 size 15° beads

figure 1

▶ **Front and Back**

1 Using size 15° beads and Delicas or Aikos, pick up 72 size 15° beads as shown in figure 1, then tie the thread to form a ring. These beads will be the first and second rows. Repeat to make a second ring—one will be the start of the front side, and the other is for the back.

2 For the front side, weave in peyote stitch until you've made 7 rows. For the back side, weave 8 rows (figure 2).

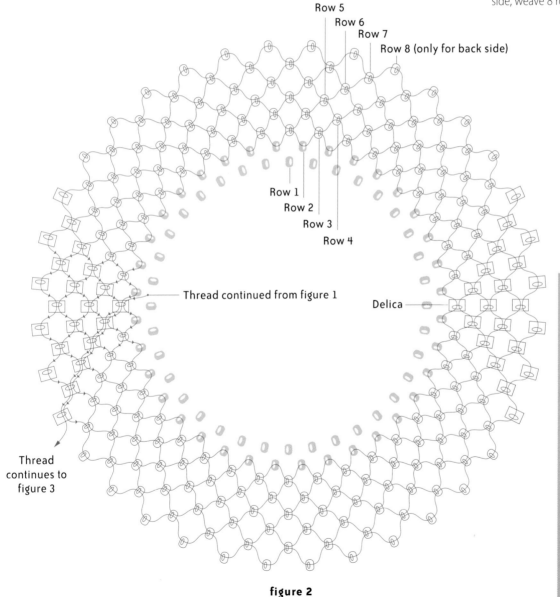

Row 5

Row 6

Row 7

Row 8 (only for back side)

Row 1

Row 2

Row 3

Row 4

Thread continued from figure 1

Delica

Thread
continues to
figure 3

figure 2

Number of beads (pick up one bead for each stitch):
Row 3: 1 Delica, 17 size 15°s, 1 Delica, and 17 size 15°s
Row 4: 1 Delica, 16 size 15°s, 2 Delicas, 16 size 15°, and 1 Delica
Row 5: 1 Delica, 15 size 15°s, 3 Delicas, 15 size 15°s, and 2 Delicas
Row 6: 1 Delica, 14 size 15°s, 4 Delicas, 14 size 15°s, and 3 Delicas
Row 7: 1 Delica, 13 size 15°s, 5 Delicas, 13 size 15°s, and 4 Delicas
Row 8: 1 Delica, 12 size 15°s, 6 Delicas, 12 size 15°s, and 5 Delicas

3 Zip the front and back sides together. As you do so, place the sew-on rhinestone inside, as shown in figure 3.

▶ Embellish

4 You'll add embellishments around the zipped area. Following figure 4, pick up size 11° beads and 3-mm bicones and weave in netting stitch, going through every single bead of Row 8 on the back side. Weave until you have three rows of netting.

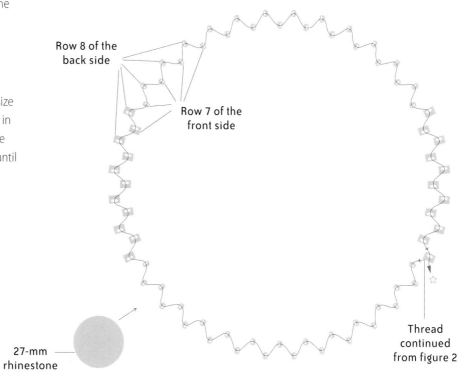

Row 8 of the back side

Row 7 of the front side

27-mm rhinestone

Thread continued from figure 2

figure 3

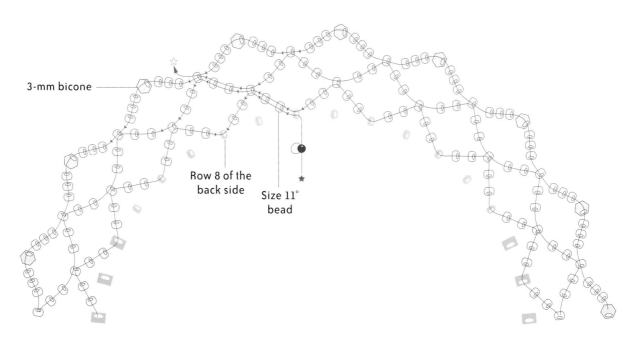

3-mm bicone

Row 8 of the back side

Size 11° bead

figure 4

5 Next, weave in netting stitch by passing through the beads in Row 7 of the back side, as shown in figure 5. Weave two rows.

6 Add more netting by going through the beads next to the ones you went through in step 5. Weave three rows (figure 6).

7 Attach the pin back to the back of the beadwork. Finish off the threads.

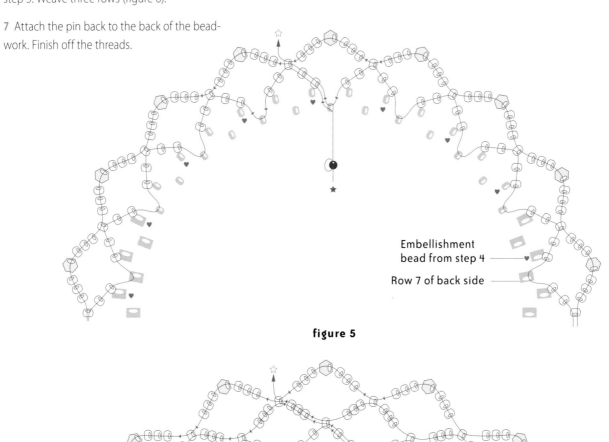

Embellishment
bead from step 4

Row 7 of back side

figure 5

Row 7 of back side

Embellishment
beads from step 5

figure 6

You don't have to make a brooch.
In the version at left, I altered
the element slightly to hang it as
a pendant. I've also made pairs
that I turned into bold earrings,
as shown in the inset.

SONOKO SPIRAL

In my second year as an instructor at the Bead&Button Show, in 2006, this necklace was the class project. You can use any palette of bead colors in this spiral rope stitch to create a unique look.

SUPPLIES

White 12° three-cut beads, 3.5 g

White 11° Aikos or Delicas, 6.5 g

Size 15° beads:

Blue, 7 g

Pink, 7 g

Gold, 3 g

Crystal bicones, 3 mm:

264 clear
(Swarovski Elements 5328, Crystal)

44 any color
(Swarovski Elements 5328)

44 any color crystal bicones, 4 mm
(Swarovski Elements 5328)

2 silver bead tips

2 silver bead caps

Silver clasp

Gray beading thread

Size 10 or 12 beading needles

Sharp snips

Glue

STITCH

Spiral Rope

FINISHED SIZE

21⅝ inches (55 cm) long

1 Pick up 4 three-cut beads as core beads, and 3 Aikos or Delicas as the spiral beads. As shown in figure 1, pass through the 4 three-cut core beads you just picked up again. Before moving on to the next step, make sure to move your spiral beads so they're on the left side of your work.

2 String 1 three-cut bead and 3 Aikos or Delicas. As shown in figure 2, pass through 4 three-cut beads again. Keep repeating this step until you have 353 spiral rows.

3 You'll embellish the top and the bottom of the spiral rows with size 15° beads. First, prepare a new thread. Start by going through the first spiral row, and weave as shown in figure 3. When you reach the end, prepare another new thread and start by going through the second spiral row. Repeat in the same way until you've embellished all the spiral rows.

4 Next, embellish the sides of the spirals. Start at the first spiral row by going through 3 Aikos or Delicas. Repeat the pattern shown in figure 4. To make the piece in your own

style, feel free to choose any color of 3-mm bicones you like, except for the clear ones.

5 Pass all the finished working threads on one end of the beadwork through a bead cap and a bead tip. On just two of those threads, add 1 Aiko or Delica, as shown in figure 5. Tie a square knot. Glue the knot, let it dry, and then close the bead tip.

6 Repeat step 5 on the other end of the beadwork. Attach one half of the clasp to one bead tip, and the other half of the clasp to the other bead tip.

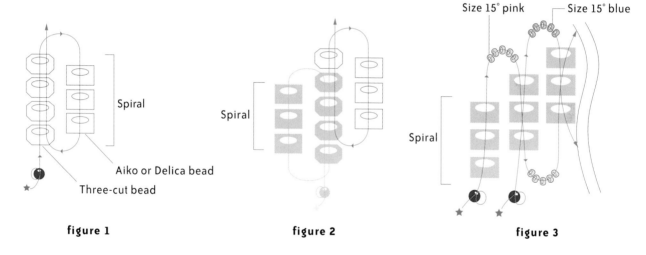

figure 1

Spiral

Aiko or Delica bead

Three-cut bead

figure 2

Spiral

figure 3

Size 15° pink   Size 15° blue

Spiral

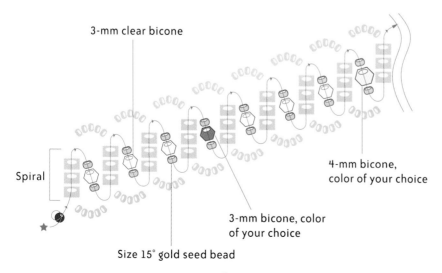

3-mm clear bicone

Spiral

4-mm bicone, color of your choice

3-mm bicone, color of your choice

Size 15° gold seed bead

figure 4

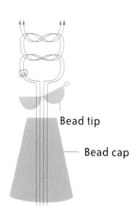

Bead tip

Bead cap

figure 5

UNDER THE SEA

This spiral rope requires much care while stitching—the thread tension must be kept soft, or else the spiral rows won't sit in the proper place. Beaded with almost 500 crystal beads, it makes a stunning necklace.

▶ Spirals

1 First, you will make a Spiral A, as shown in figure 1. Pick up 3 size 6° beads for the core and the other beads for the spiral. Pass through the 3 size 6° beads again, as shown in the illustration. Before moving on to the next step, push the spiral beads to the left.

2 Pick up 1 size 6° bead and the spiral beads shown in figure 2. Pass through 3 size 6° core beads as shown in the illustration. Repeat this step until you have 172 spiral rows.

3 Next, make Spiral Bs opposite the Spiral As so both kinds share the core beads. (Figure 3 shows only Spiral B.) Just like in steps 1 and 2, repeat the spiral stitch along the entire length of the beadwork, passing through 3 core size 6° beads for each spiral row. This time, push the spiral beads to the right side.

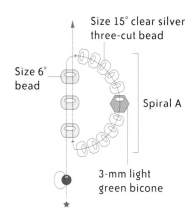

Size 15° clear silver three-cut bead

Size 6° bead

Spiral A

3-mm light green bicone

figure 1

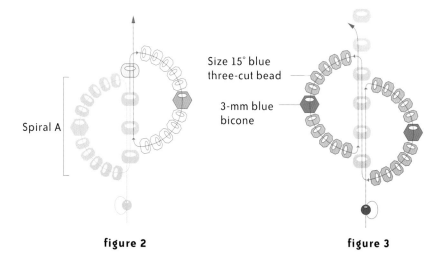

Spiral A

Size 15° blue three-cut bead

3-mm blue bicone

figure 2

figure 3

SUPPLIES

Size 6° light blue beads, 17 g

Size 15° three-cut beads:

  Clear silver, 9 g

  Blue, 9 g

Crystal bicones, 3 mm:

  172 light green (Swarovski Elements 5328, Lime)

  172 blue (Swarovski Elements 5328, Indigo Light)

  145 clear (Swarovski Elements 5328, Crystal)

Size 11° turquoise blue beads, 9 g

29 gold glass pearls, 3 mm (Swarovski Elements 5810, Gold)

2 size 11° Aikos or Delicas

2 silver bead tips

2 silver bead caps

Silver clasp

Gray beading thread

Size 10 or 12 beading needles

Sharp snips

Glue

STITCH

Spiral Rope

FINISHED SIZE

23⅝ inches (60 cm) long

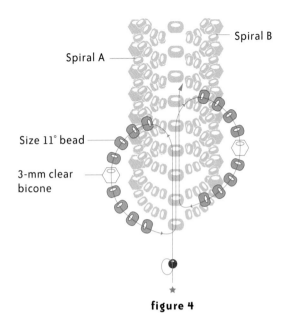

Spiral B

Spiral A

Size 11° bead

3-mm clear
bicone

figure 4

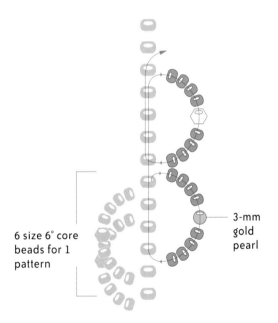

6 size 6° core
beads for 1
pattern

3-mm
gold
pearl

figure 5

4 Make two Spiral Cs, as shown in figure 4. First, open the A and B Spirals so you can see the core beads. With a new thread, pass through 4 size 6° core beads and pick up size 11° beads and a 3-mm bicone for the spiral. This is Spiral C, Row 1. Next, pass through 5 size 6° core beads. Now turn the spiral beads to the left. Pick up spiral beads for Row 2 and go through 5 size 6° core beads, as shown in the illustration. Make sure your spiral beads are on the left side.

5 For Spiral C, Row 3, pick up size 11° beads and a 3-mm glass pearl. (Figure 5 shows only Spiral C.) Pass through 8 size 6° core beads and turn the spiral beads to the left. Repeat steps 4 and 5 until you have 87 spiral rows (or 29 patterns).

6 Make Spiral Ds, as shown in figure 6. First, turn over your spiral rope. Open Spirals A and B to see the core beads. Repeat steps 4 and 5, but this time use size 11° beads and clear 3-mm bicones for the spiral rows.

▶ **Finish**

7 On one end of the rope, pass all the remaining threads through a bead cap and a bead tip. Divide these threads into two groups of two (as shown in figure 7), and put a pair of the threads through an Aiko or Delica. Tie a square knot and glue it. Close the bead tip.

8 Repeat step 7 on the other end of the rope. Attach one-half of the clasp to each of the bead tips.

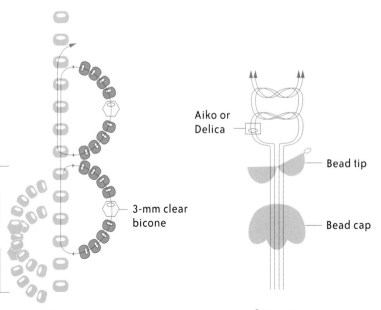

6 size 6° core
beads for 1
pattern

3-mm clear
bicone

Aiko or
Delica

Bead tip

Bead cap

figure 6   **figure 7**

SONOKO WAVE

To create this fanciful piece, I invented a technique based on peyote stitch.

This method forms a lovely spiral without the use of embedded wire.

SUPPLIES

Size 15° silver beads, 7.5 g

Size 11° gold beads, 3.6 g

190 green AB crystal bicones, 3 mm
(Swarovski Elements 5328)

2 gold bead caps

1 gold toggle clasp

Gray beading thread

Size 10 or 12 beading needles

Sharp snips

4 feet (1.2 m) of nylon thread,
0.8 mm diameter

STITCH

Peyote

FINISHED SIZE

15 inches (38 cm) long

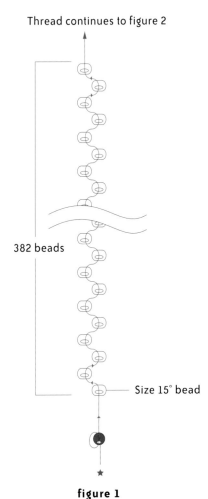

Thread continues to figure 2

382 beads

Size 15° bead

figure 1

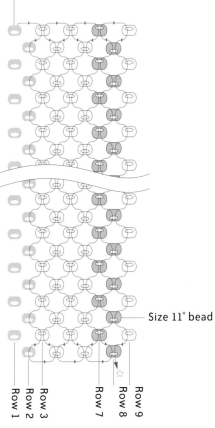

Thread continued from figure 1

Size 11° bead

Row 1
Row 2
Row 3
Row 7
Row 8
Row 9

figure 2

1 Using beading thread, pick up 382 size 15° beads, as shown in figure 1. These beads will become rows 1 and 2.

2 Weave in peyote stitch (as shown in figure 2), using size 15° beads for rows 3 to 6, size 11° beads for rows 7 and 8, and size 15° beads for row 9. When you stitch with the size 11° beads, your work will start spiraling.

3 Using the nylon thread, form the bead-work into a tube by zipping up rows 1 and 9, picking up a 3-mm bicone between beads as shown in figure 3.

4 On each end of the tube, pass the remaining threads through a bead cap, size 15° beads, half of the toggle clasp, more 15° beads, and then through the bead cap again, as shown in figure 4, then finish off the threads.

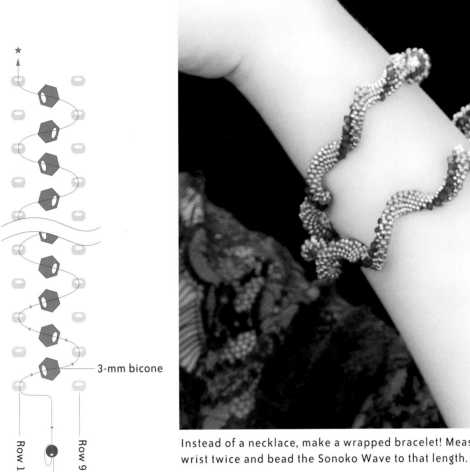

3-mm bicone

Row 1

Row 9

figure 3

Instead of a necklace, make a wrapped bracelet! Measure loosely around your wrist twice and bead the Sonoko Wave to that length.

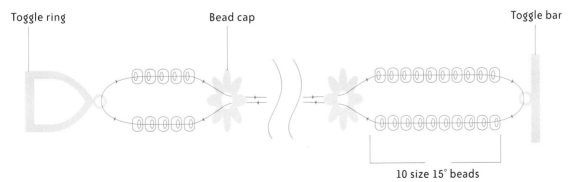

Toggle ring

Bead cap

Toggle bar

10 size 15° beads

figure 4

CHAPTER 4
ELEGANT

These shiny, colorful pieces are wearable, stylish, and chic.

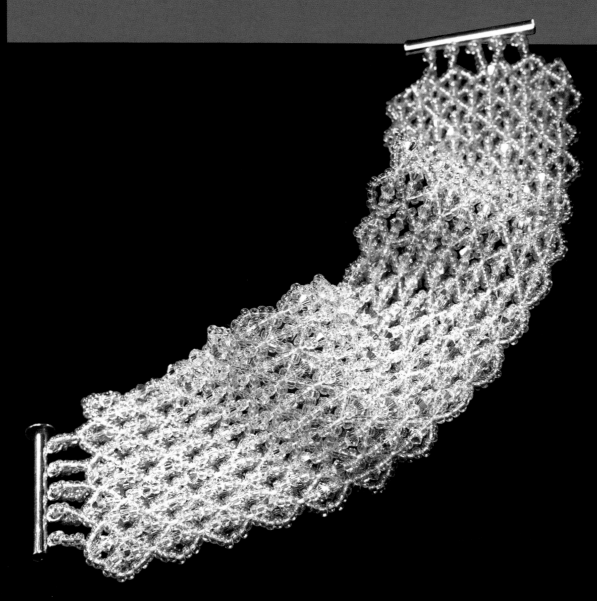

NIGHT DEW

This reversible bracelet, woven in netting stitch, features shimmering bicones. One side uses AB crystals and the other a solid color, giving you two different ways to wear it.

SUPPLIES

Size 11° clear beads, 20 g

Size 15° clear beads, 3 g

Crystal bicones, 3 mm:

170 clear AB (Swarovski Elements 5328, Crystal AB)

170 pale blue (Swarovski Elements 5328, Aquamarine)

1 silver five-strand magnetic clasp

White beading thread

Size 10 or 12 beading needles

Sharp snips

STITCH

Netting

FINISHED SIZE

8⅝ inches (22 cm) long

▶ Base

1 Pick up size 11° beads and weave in netting stitch for 5 rows, following figure 1.

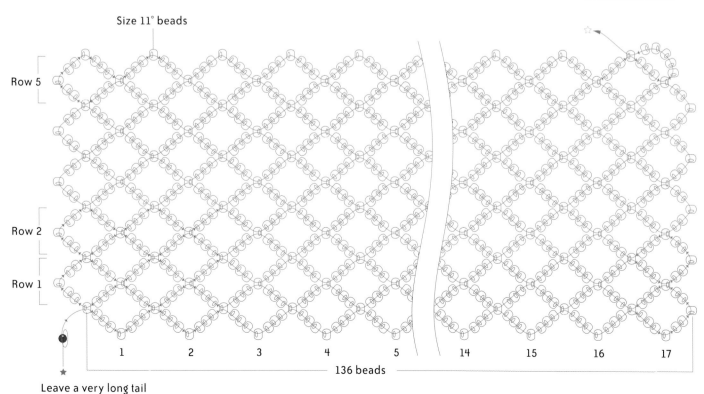

Size 11° beads

Row 5

Row 2

Row 1

Leave a very long tail

1   2   3   4   5   14   15   16   17

— 136 beads —

figure 1

2 Using the tail thread, pick up size 11° beads and go through the bead in the base, as shown in figure 2.

▶ Embellish

3 You'll embellish both the front and the back sides of the base as follows, using the clear AB bicones for the front and the pale blue bicones for the back. First, pass through a size 11° bead of the base, as shown in figure 3. Pick up 1 size 15° bead, 1 size 11° bead, one 3-mm bicone, 1 size 11° bead, and 1 size 15° bead.

▶ Finish

4 Attach the two parts of the clasp by passing through the base beads and picking up new size 11° beads, as shown in figure 4.

5 Weave back into the base and finish off the threads.

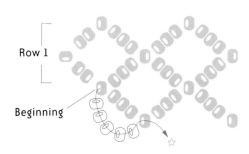

Row 1

Beginning

figure 2

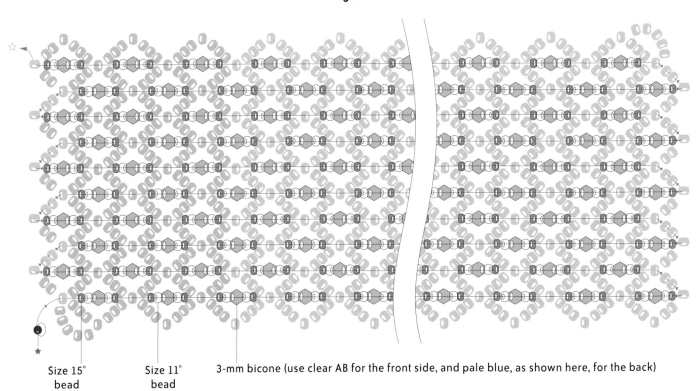

Size 15° bead

Size 11° bead

3-mm bicone (use clear AB for the front side, and pale blue, as shown here, for the back)

figure 3

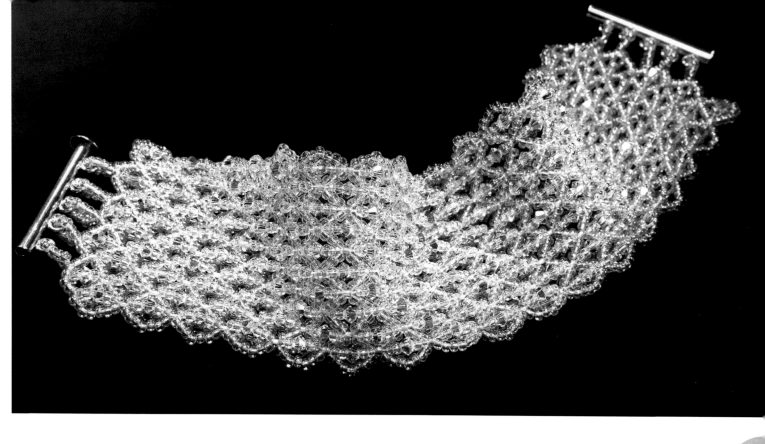

figure 4

BEACH AT NIGHT

Woven in chevron stitch, this necklace is made with rhodium beads.

They lend a moderate weight along with a solid metallic quality.

1 Weave two strands in chevron stitch, following figure 1. Make one strand 17¾ inches (45.1 cm) long, using 15° silver metal beads and gold round metal beads and a thread color that's the best match. Make the other strand 15¾ inches long (40 cm), with black metal beads and silver round metal beads and the best match of thread.

2 Attach the clasp by catching it in loops of round metal beads added through the threads of the beginning and end of each strand, as shown in figure 2. Weave back in and finish off the threads.

SUPPLIES

Size 15° metal beads:

Silver, 7.5 g

Black, 5 g

Size 18° round metal beads:

Gold, 1.7 g

Silver, 1.5 g

1 silver two-strand magnetic clasp

Black and gray beading threads

Size 10 or 12 beading needles

Sharp snips

STITCH

Chevron

FINISHED SIZE

15¾ inches (40 cm) long

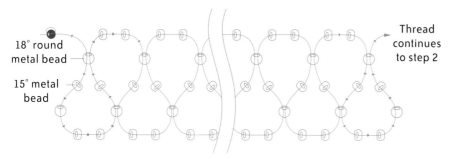

18° round metal bead

15° metal bead

Thread continues to step 2

figure 1

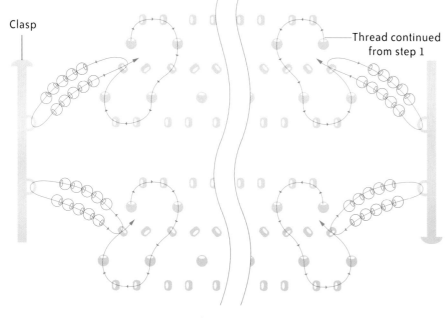

Clasp

Thread continued from step 1

figure 2

AURORA

White is my favorite color, so I chose to feature it in this necklace. I sought to express a profound design by using Toho glass pearls and crystal beads.

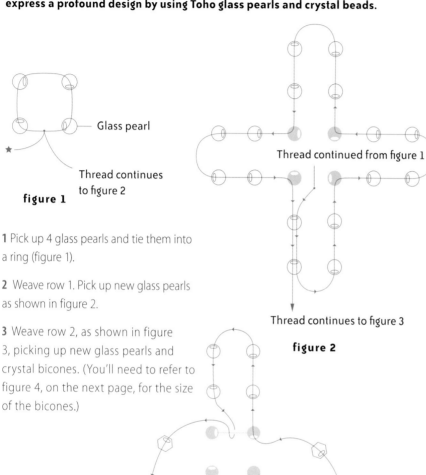

Glass pearl

Thread continues to figure 2

figure 1

Thread continued from figure 1

Thread continues to figure 3

figure 2

Thread continued from figure 2

Crystal bicone

Thread continues to figure 5

figure 3

1 Pick up 4 glass pearls and tie them into a ring (figure 1).

2 Weave row 1. Pick up new glass pearls as shown in figure 2.

3 Weave row 2, as shown in figure 3, picking up new glass pearls and crystal bicones. (You'll need to refer to figure 4, on the next page, for the size of the bicones.)

SUPPLIES

1468 ivory glass pearls, 2 mm

Crystal bicones:

216 clear AB, 3 mm (Swarovski Elements 5328, Crystal AB)

140 clear AB, 4 mm (Swarovski Elements 5328, Crystal AB)

Silver cameo clasp

White beading thread

Size 10 or 12 beading needles

Sharp snips

STITCH

Zulu

FINISHED SIZE

16½ inches (41.9 cm) long

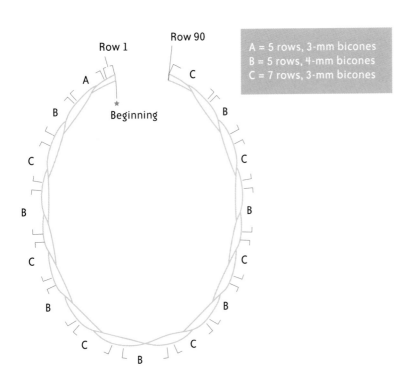

Row 1

Row 90

A = 5 rows, 3-mm bicones
B = 5 rows, 4-mm bicones
C = 7 rows, 3-mm bicones

A

C

B

B

★ Beginning

C

C

B

B

C

C

B

B

C

C

B

figure 4

4 Figure 4 is a schematic of the bead weaving for the entire length of the necklace. Weave in the same way as for row 2 until you have 90 rows. Be careful to select the correct sizes of bicones.

5 For the last row, pick up 4 glass pearls, as shown in figure 5.

6 As shown in figure 6, string glass pearls at both the beginning and end of the piece, attaching each part of the clasp into one of those loops. Weave back into your work and finish off all threads.

68

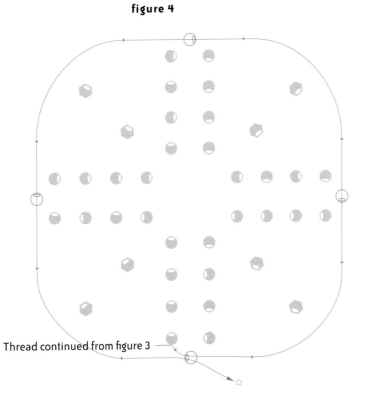

Thread continued from figure 3

figure 5

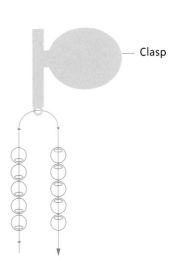

Clasp

figure 6

LILY

These earrings are inspired by the shape of the lily flower. Petal-like parts are woven with seed beads, and the crystal drop beads are wrapped with them.

SUPPLIES

148 white 11° Delicas

132 crystal AB faceted round crystal beads, 2 mm (Swarovski Elements 5000, Crystal AB)

30 size 15° gold seed beads

2 crystal AB briolette pendants, 11 x 5.5 mm (Swarovski Elements 6010, Crystal AB)

2 gold bead caps

2 gold earring findings

White beading thread

Size 10 or 12 beading needles

Sharp snips

STITCH

Brick

FINISHED SIZE

1 inch (2.5 cm) long

1 Using Delicas and following figure 1, weave 7 rows in double ladder stitch, a variation of brick stitch. When you finish the seventh row, pass through the first 2 beads again to make a tube.

2 Keep weaving in the round using two-drop brick stitch (which is done by picking up 2 beads per stitch instead of 1) until you have 4 rows, increasing as you go, as shown in figure 2.

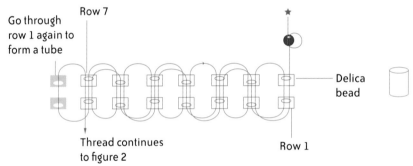

Go through row 1 again to form a tube

Row 7

★

Delica bead

Thread continues to figure 2

Row 1

figure 1

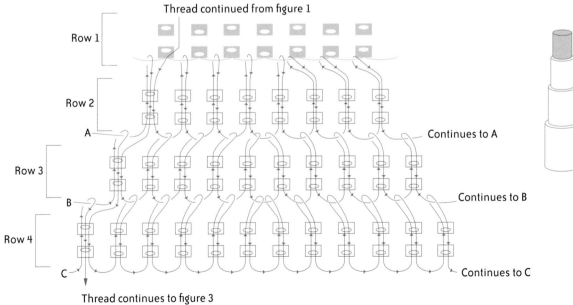

Thread continued from figure 1

Row 1

Row 2

A

Continues to A

Row 3

B

Continues to B

Row 4

C

Continues to C

Thread continues to figure 3

figure 2

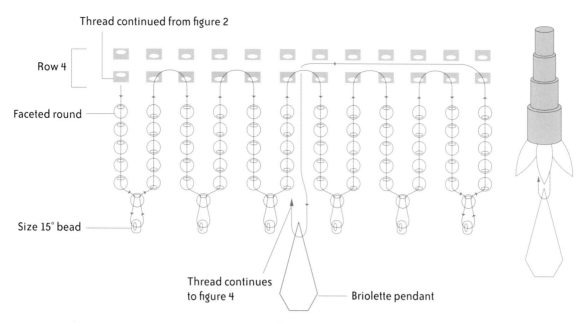

Thread continued from figure 2

Row 4

Faceted round

Size 15° bead

Thread continues to figure 4

Briolette pendant

figure 3

3 Pick up 6 faceted rounds and 1 size 15° bead. Pass back through the sixth faceted round again. Pick up 5 more faceted rounds and pass through one Delica in your work. Repeat this around, as shown in figure 3. Next, pick up 1 briolette pendant. Pass the thread through the bead in row 1, and pass back through the briolette pendant again.

4 Pass through the tube and come out from the Delica in row 1. As shown in figure 4, pick up a bead cap, size 15° beads, an earring finding, and additional 15° beads. Pass back through the bead cap again and then pass through the next Delica bead in row 1.

5 Pass through all the beads you picked up in step 4, then pass back into the next Delica bead. Repeat this all the way around by passing through Delicas, from 1 to 7, as shown in figure 5. Finish off the threads.

6 Repeat all the steps to make a second earring.

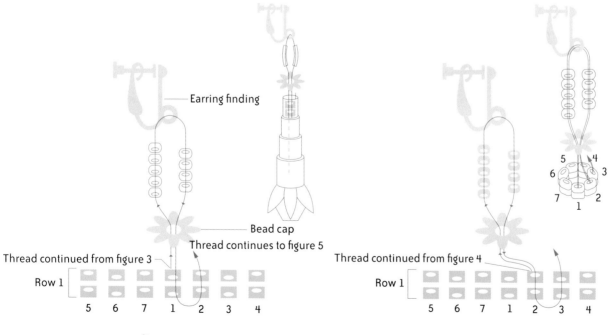

Earring finding

Bead cap
Thread continues to figure 5

Thread continued from figure 3

Row 1

5   6   7   1   2   3   4

figure 4

Thread continued from figure 4

Row 1

5   6   7   1   2   3   4

5   4
6   3
7   2
1

figure 5

BREATH
OF SPRING

To allow the fringe of this scarf-like necklace to lie in a way that shows it off properly, I chose beads with some weight. I recommend using Miyuki's seed beads for the fringe, because they're slightly heavier than beads made by other manufacturers.

SUPPLIES

Size 6° white beads, 26 g

Size 15° green three-cut beads, 20 g

Crystal bicones, 3 mm:

330 yellow-green (Swarovski Elements 5328, Peridot)

332 palest gray (Swarovski Element 5328, Crystal Satin)

56 pale yellow (Swarovski Elements 5328, Jonquil)

332 clear (Swarovski Elements 5328, Crystal)

56 violet (Swarovski Elements 5328, Violet)

Size 15° beads:

White, 29 g

Silver, 28 g

Pearl white, 5 g

Purple, 5 g

Translucent white, 10 g

35 crystal flower beads, 5 mm:

Clear AB (Swarovski Elements 5744, Crystal AB)

Yellow-green (Swarovski Elements 5744, Peridot)

Light blue (Swarovski Elements 5744, Aquamarine)

Pink (Swarovski Elements 5744, Light Rose)

2 purple briolette pendants, 17 x 8.5 mm (Swarovski Elements 6010)

Gray beading thread

Size 10 or 12 beading needles

Sharp snips

STITCH

Spiral Rope

FINISHED SIZE

39³/₈ inches (100 cm) long

► Rope

1 Make a length of beadwork as follows. As shown in figure 1, pick up 4 size 6° beads for the core, and size 15° three-cut beads and a yellow-green bicone for the spiral. Pass through the 4 size 6° beads again. Before moving on to the next step, push your spiral beads to the left.

2 Referring to figure 2, pick up 1 size 6° bead for the core, and three-cut beads and a 3-mm bicone for the spiral, then pass through 4 size 6° beads again. Repeat this until you've beaded 330 spiral rows.

► Fringe

3 Add fringe A, shown in figure 3, at the bottom of each spiral woven in steps 1 and 2. Following the illustration, go through 1 core size 6° bead. Pick up 18 size 15° beads, a 3-mm bicone, and a white 15° for each strand of fringe. Go back through the bicone and the 15°s of the fringe, and through the next core size 6° bead. You'll attach a total of 332 fringe As.

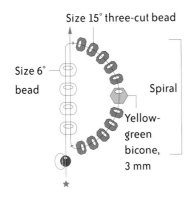

Size 15° three-cut bead

Size 6° bead

Spiral

Yellow-green bicone, 3 mm

figure 1

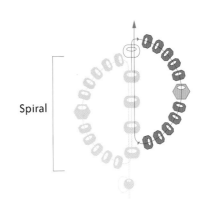

Spiral

figure 2

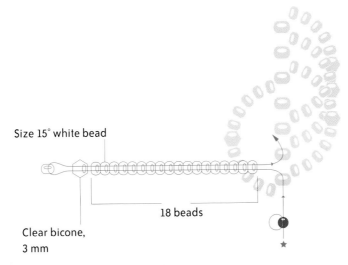

Size 15° white bead

Clear bicone, 3 mm

18 beads

figure 3

4 Much as you did in step 3, add fringe B (shown in figure 4) at the bottoms of all the spirals, attaching a total of 332 fringes. Starting with a new thread, use 18 silver 15°s, a 3-mm palest gray bicone, and a silver 15° for each fringe B.

5 Refer to figure 5 for fringe placement as you do steps 5 through 7. Note that the fringes will achieve better balance if you add fringe C to the side of fringe B and fringe D to the side of fringe C.

Add 28 fringe Cs near each end of the rope; a fringe C consists of 20 pearl white 15°s, a 3-mm pale yellow bicone, and a pearl white 15°.

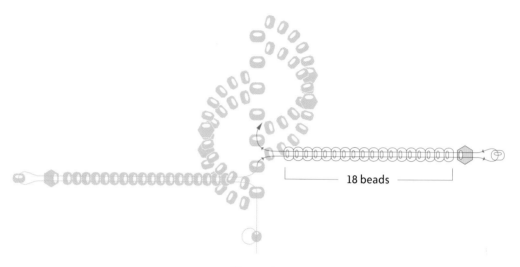

18 beads

figure 4

a: Add 332 each of fringes A and B along the entire length.
Fringe A (332 fringes) = 18 white 15°s, 1 clear bicone, 1 white 15°
Fringe B (332 fringes) = 14 silver 15°s, 1 palest gray bicone, 1 silver 15°
b: Fringe D (56 fringes at the beginning of the foundation) = 20 purple 15°s, 1 violet bicone, 1 purple 15°
c: Fringe C (28 fringes at both the beginning and ending) = 20 pearl white 15°s, 1 pale yellow bicone, 1 pearl white 15°
d: Fringe E (35 fringes at the beginning of the necklace) = 20 size 15° translucent white, 1 flower bead, and 20 size 15° translucent white

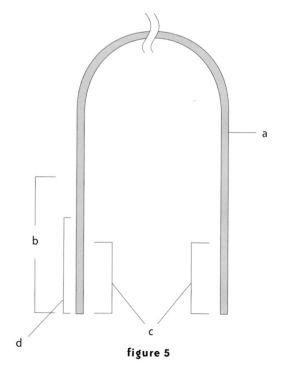

figure 5

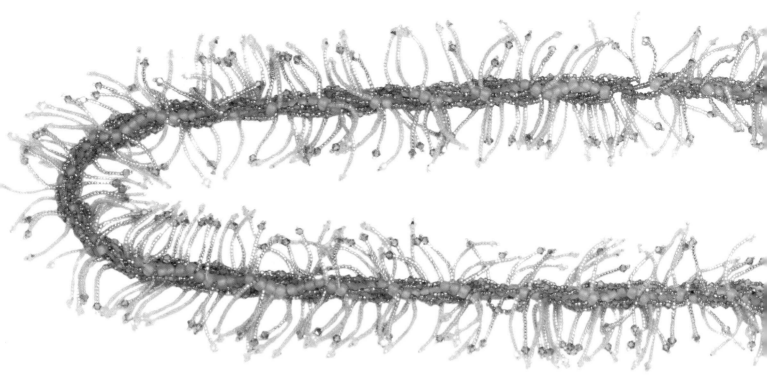

6 Next, add 56 fringe Ds to the beginning of the rope, making each from 20 purple 15°s, a 3-mm violet bicone, and a purple 15°.

7 Add 35 fringe Es to the beginning of the necklace, each one a loop made from translucent white 15°s and flower beads, as shown in figure 6. Attach fringe E to the rope and come out from the side of fringe D.

8 As shown in figure 7, pass your threads through size 15° beads and a briolette pendant at both the beginning and ending of the rope. Weave back in and finish off the threads.

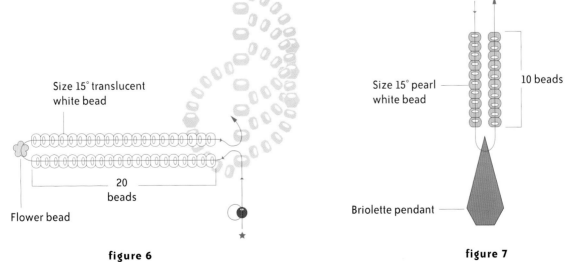

Size 15° translucent white bead

Flower bead

20 beads

figure 6

Size 15° pearl white bead

10 beads

Briolette pendant

figure 7

MILKY WAY

Using size 15° beads and crystals, this necklace is stitched with a unique technique that resembles peyote. It's very comfortable to wear and looks great in all kinds of social settings.

1 String size 15°s on a thread until the combined beads measure 15¾ inches (40.6 cm), as shown in figure 1. These beads will become rows 1 and 2.

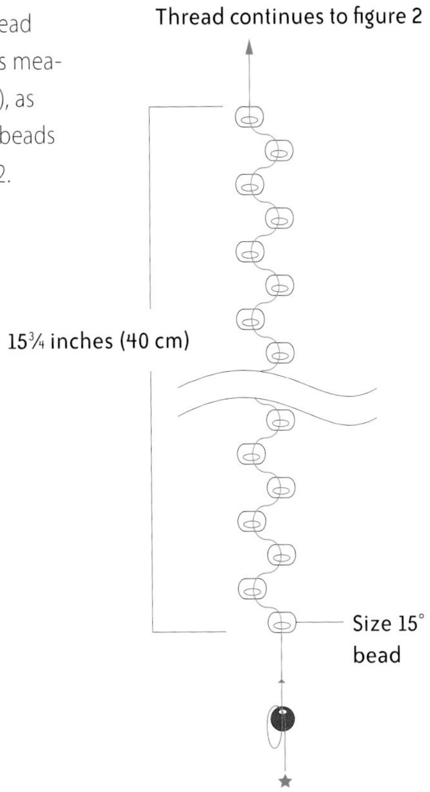

Thread continues to figure 2

15¾ inches (40 cm)

Size 15° bead

figure 1

2 Using peyote stitch, weave 8 rows with size 15° beads and 4 rows with charlotte beads, for a total of 12 rows. Zip the beads in row 12 and row 1 to make a tube. Come out from bead A (figure 2).

▶ **Embellish**

3 Using a new thread and exiting from a charlotte bead in row 9, pick up 1 charlotte, one 5-mm flower bead, and 1 charlotte, as shown in figure 3. Then go back through the charlotte in the beadwork again to attach the embellishment. Repeat for the diagonally adjacent charlotte beads in row 10 and row 9.

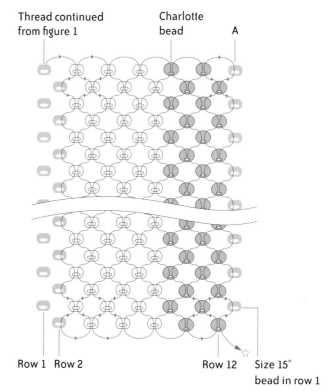

Thread continued from figure 1

Charlotte bead

A

Row 1　Row 2

Row 12

Size 15° bead in row 1

figure 2

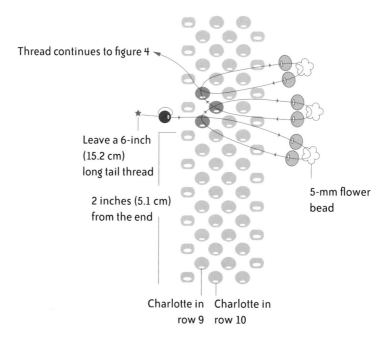

Thread continues to figure 4

Leave a 6-inch (15.2 cm) long tail thread

2 inches (5.1 cm) from the end

5-mm flower bead

Charlotte in row 9　　Charlotte in row 10

figure 3

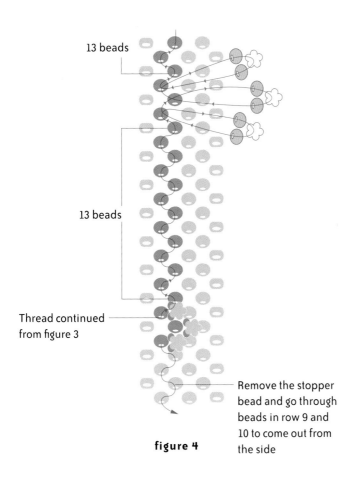

13 beads

13 beads

Thread continued
from figure 3

Remove the stopper
bead and go through
beads in row 9 and
10 to come out from
the side

figure 4

4 Move your thread by passing through 13 charlottes each in rows 9 and 10. Then continue adding embellishments as done previously. Repeat until you've added three embellishments in 16 places on the work. Weave both beginning and ending threads to come out from the side bead by going through the charlottes in rows 9 and 10 (figure 4).

▶ **Finish**

5 Pass the remaining thread on one end through a bead cap and bead tip. Pick up an Aiko or Delica bead, tie a square knot, and glue it (figure 5). Close the bead tip. Repeat on the other end of the beadwork. Attach each half of the clasp to one of the bead tips.

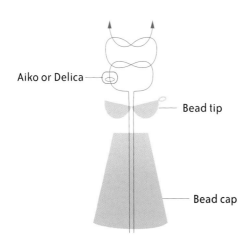

Aiko or Delica

Bead tip

Bead cap

figure 5

NOBLE

These jewelry pieces are created with simple colors,

giving them a clean, neat quality and an air of refinement.

SNOW WHITE

I chose spiral rope stitch when I thought up a new design in basic white. By stitching with three beads of different textures, the natural color gradations create a lovely effect.

SUPPLIES

Size 8° white beads, 3.5 g

Size 11° beads:

Silver, 3 g

Clear, 15 g

Matte white, 15 g

Crystal bicones, 3 mm:

532 clear (Swarovski Elements 5328, Crystal)

138 clear AB (Swarovski Elements 5328, Crystal AB)

Silver clasp

Gray beading thread

Size 10 or 12 beading needles

Sharp snips

STITCH

Spiral Rope

FINISHED SIZE

17³/₈ inches (44 cm) long

▶ Spirals

1 Following figure 1, pick up 4 size 8° beads for the core and the indicated size 11° silver and clear beads for the spiral. As shown in the diagram, pass through all 4 size 8° beads again. Finally, before moving on to the next step, push the beads in your spiral to the left side of your work.

2 As shown in figure 2, pick up 1 size 8° bead, along with the indicated size 11° silver and clear beads for the spiral. Pass through 4 size 8° beads again. Repeat until you have 137 spiral rows.

▶ Add Color

3 Next, you'll make new spiral rows in different colors, adding them so they share the existing core beads. Go through the 4 core size 8° beads you picked up in step 1. Pick up the spiral beads and come out through the fifth bead from the bottom. Repeat this step for all 137 spirals while going through 4 core beads for each stitch, as shown in figure 3.

▶ Add Crystal Beads

4 The next step is to make additional spiral rows with bicones. Go through 3 of the core size 8° beads you picked up in step 1 again. Pick up crystal beads (as shown in figure 4) and come out from the fourth bead from the bottom.

5 Repeat step 4 until you've woven 138 spiral rows, arranging the colors as desired by stringing on the AB crystals in different places.

▶ Finish

6 When you reach the end, string size 11° beads through the three threads coming out from the last 8° bead, then one half of the clasp, and more size 11° beads, as shown in figure 5. Tie several half-hitch knots, then cut all threads off. Repeat on the other end of the necklace to attach the other half of the clasp.

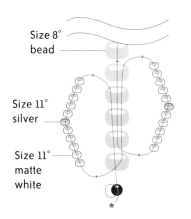

figure 1

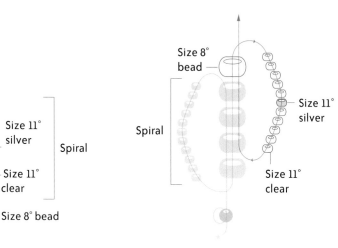

figure 2

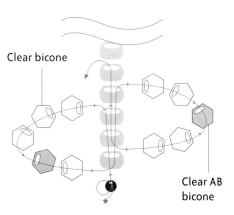

Clear bicone

Clear AB bicone

figure 4

Size 8° bead

Size 11° silver

Size 11° matte white

figure 3

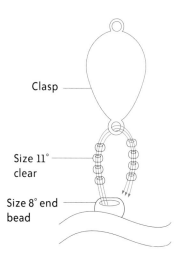

Clasp

Size 11° clear

Size 8° end bead

figure 5

SUPPLIES

Size 15° beads:

   Gold, 2.5g

   Silver, 2.5g

**334 black faceted crystal rounds, 2 mm
(Swarovski Elements 5000, Jet)**

Two 11° Aikos or Delicas, any color

2 gold bead caps

2 gold bead tips

Gold clasp

Glue

Gray beading thread

Size 10 or 12 beading needles

Sharp snips

STITCH

Chevron

FINISHED SIZE

16½ inches (42 cm) long

MIDNIGHT

This necklace, woven in chevron stitch, has a flexible, comfortable feel. You can produce a smooth texture with this stitch as long as you use beads no larger than 2 mm.

Black crystal round

Size 15° silver

Size 15° gold

1   2   3   110   111

Row 1

Row 2

Row 3

Share crystal rounds with row 1

1   2   3   110   111

figure 1

1 With a thread 110 inches (279.4 cm) long, weave the first row in chevron stitch, as shown in figure 1. With a new thread, weave a second row that shares its crystal rounds with the first row. For the third row, pick up size 15° beads as shown and share crystal rounds with the first and second rows, forming a tube.

2 As shown in figure 2, pass all three threads on one side of the beadwork through a bead cap and a bead tip. Divide these threads into two and one, and put 1 Aiko or Delica through the two threads. Tie a square knot. Glue it and let it dry. Close the bead tip. Repeat this step on the other end of the piece, using the other bead cap and tip.

3 Attach one half of the clasp to each of the bead tips. With a new thread, pass through the finished necklace to tighten your work.

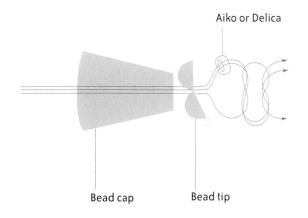

Aiko or Delica

Bead cap

Bead tip

figure 2

POWDER SNOW

Netted bracelets are comfortable to wear, fitting easily around your wrist. I selected metal beads that would add a different texture to the beautiful glass pearls.

SUPPLIES*

84 white glass pearls, 4 mm
(Swarovski Elements 5810, White)

Size 11° beads:

Silver, 4.5 g

Gold, 0.5 g

1 three-strand silver magnetic clasp

White beading thread

Size 10 or 12 beading needles

Sharp snips

* To make the bracelet as shown in
the foreground.

STITCH

Netting

FINISHED SIZE

7¾ inches (20 cm) long

1 The supplies listed are enough to make one bracelet. You'll begin by making one row going to each hole of the clasp, using one thread for each row, as shown in figure 1. Weave 21 glass pearls in each row, using netting stitch and sharing beads between rows.

2 Tie several half-hitch knots in the finished bracelet and finish off the threads.

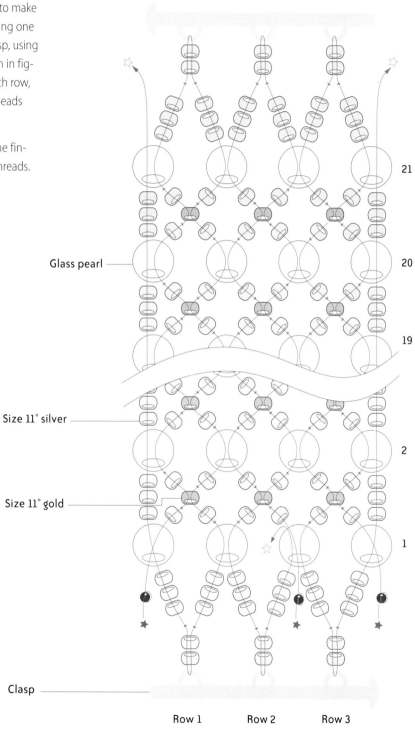

Glass pearl

21

20

19

Size 11° silver

2

Size 11° gold

1

Clasp

Row 1   Row 2   Row 3

figure 1

MORNING GLOW

I like to wear this charm as a sash clip or as a pendant, but you could turn it into a brooch or even a hair ornament. I bezel a large cabochon with seed beads, and then, to make it more striking, add a frilled embellishment around it.

SUPPLIES

Size 15° gold beads, 2.2 g

Gold 11° Delicas, 0.4 g

1 malachite cabochon, 5 x 15 x 20 mm

Size 11° gold beads, 0.2 g

40 clear round faceted crystal beads, 2 mm (Swarovski Elements 5000, Crystal)

Beige beading thread

Size 10 or 12 beading needles

Sharp snips

STITCH

Peyote

FINISHED SIZE

1³/₈ x 1⁹/₁₆ inches (3.5 x 4 cm)

► Bezel

1 Pick up 40 size 15° beads and tie the thread to form a ring (figure 1). These will become rows 1 and 2.

2 Using peyote stitch and following figure 2, weave 4 rows with size 15° beads, 5 rows with Delicas—put in the cabochon, face up, after completing the fifth row of Delicas—and 2 rows with size 15° beads. Keep stitching with Delicas and size 15° beads to bezel the stone. (Be careful that the beginning goes to the back side.)

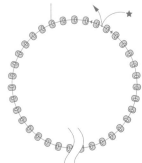

40 size 15° beads   Thread continues to next figure

figure 1

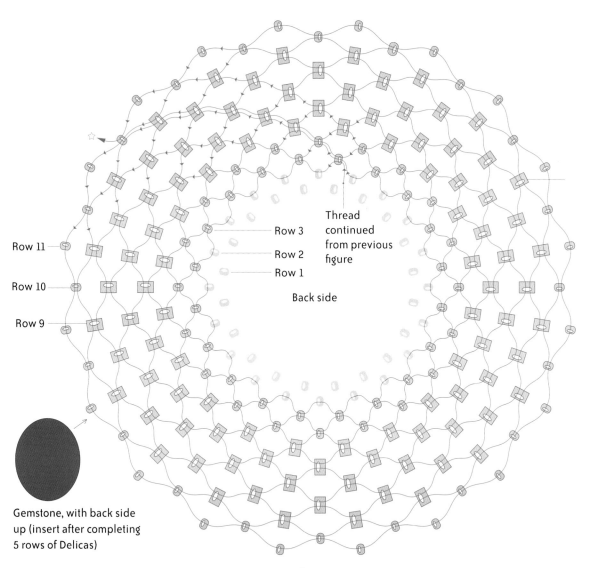

Row 11

Row 10

Row 9

Row 3

Row 2

Row 1

Thread continued from previous figure

Back side

Gemstone, with back side up (insert after completing 5 rows of Delicas)

figure 2

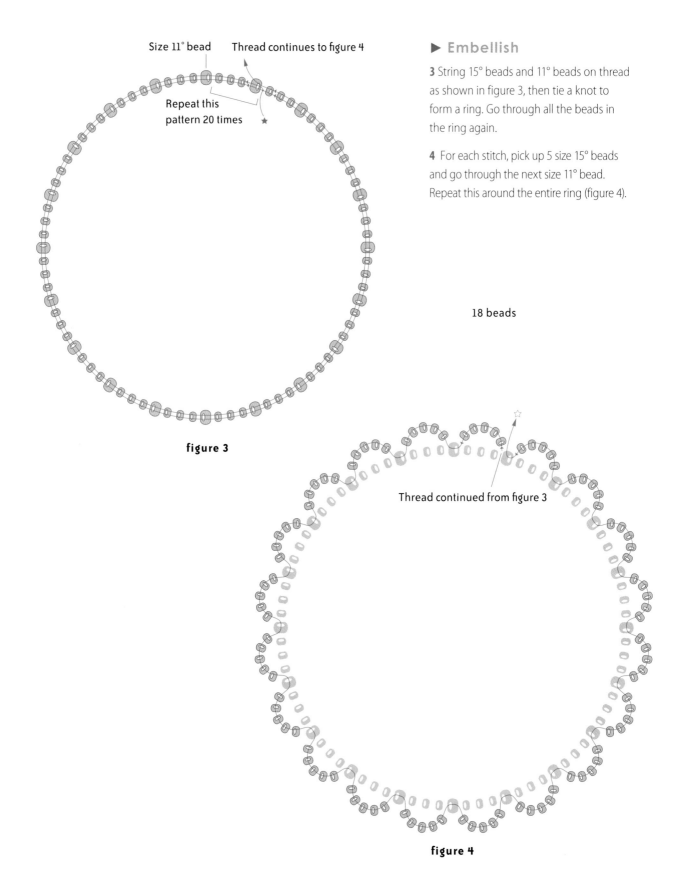

Size 11° bead   Thread continues to figure 4

Repeat this
pattern 20 times   ★

figure 3

▶ Embellish

3 String 15° beads and 11° beads on thread
as shown in figure 3, then tie a knot to
form a ring. Go through all the beads in
the ring again.

4 For each stitch, pick up 5 size 15° beads
and go through the next size 11° bead.
Repeat this around the entire ring (figure 4).

18 beads

Thread continued from figure 3

figure 4

► Assemble

5 To join the bezeled element and the embellishment, add a new thread exiting from the bead in row 9 of the bezel. (It's the third row when you count from the center front.) As shown in figure 5, pick up size 15° beads and 2-mm round crystal beads and go through the size 11° beads of the embellishment. Repeat this around the entire ring. Finish off the threads.

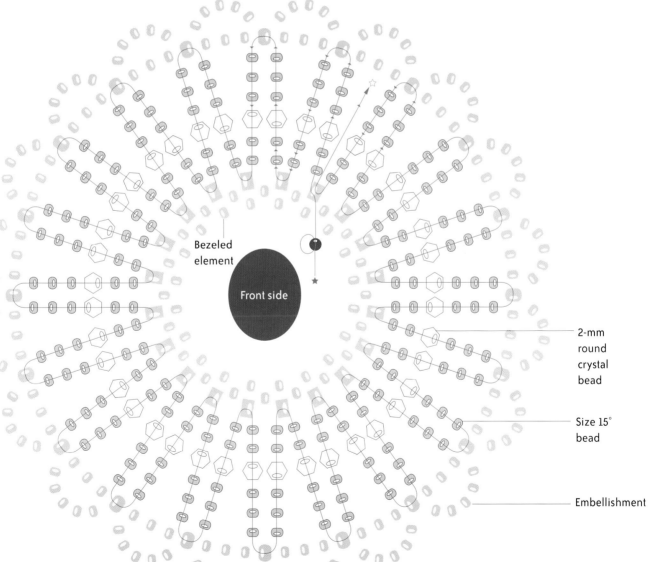

Bezeled element

Front side

2-mm round crystal bead

Size 15° bead

Embellishment

figure 5

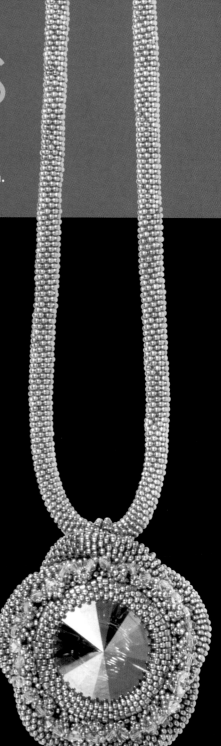

CHAPTER 6
GORGEOUS

Any of these glamorous pieces would make the perfect

accessory for dressing up an outfit for a night on the town.

SOUND OF RAINDROPS

This necklace consists of a rope laced through several frilly charms. (A single, unattached charm is shown in the center of the photo at left.) You can add as many or as few charms as you like. While their volume makes the necklace look heavy, this piece is actually very light and easy to wear.

▶ Rope

1 Pick up 4 Aiko or Delica beads for the core, and size 15° beads for the spiral, as shown in figure 1. Pass through the 4 Aikos or Delicas. Before moving on to the next step, move your spiral beads to the left side of your work.

2 Pick up 1 Aiko or Delica and 3 silver size 15° beads for the spiral (figure 2). Then pass through 4 Aikos or Delicas as shown. Repeat this step until the rope you've beaded measures 16½ inches (42 cm).

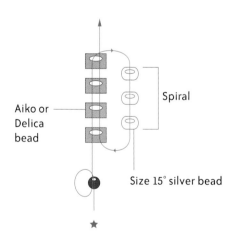

Aiko or Delica bead — Spiral — Size 15° silver bead

figure 1

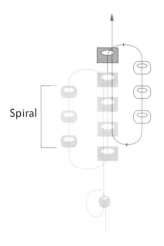

Spiral

figure 2

SUPPLIES

Silver 11° Aikos or Delicas, 2.4 g

Size 15° beads:

   Silver, 3.5 g

   Clear silver, 3.3 g

Size 13° clear charlotte beads, 7 g

Size 10° antique silver Matsunos, 7 g

Blue-gold triangle beads, 27 g

2 silver bead tips

2 silver bead caps

Silver clasp

White beading thread

Size 10 or 12 beading needles

Sharp snips

Glue

STITCHES

Spiral Rope

Peyote

FINISHED SIZE

16½ inches (42 cm) long

► Embellish

3 Use size 15° beads to add embellishments on the tops and bottoms of all the spirals, as shown in figure 3. Pass through the first spiral beads, then pick up new size 15° beads. Weave in a zigzag.

4 Next, with a new thread, start by passing through the second spiral row. Add extra embellishments, alternating with those from step 3, as shown in figure 4.

► Clasp

5 Pass all the remaining threads on one end of the rope through a bead cap and a bead tip. Divide them into a pair of two threads and a single one, then put an Aiko or Delica through the pair of threads, as shown in figure 5. Tie a square knot and glue it. Close the bead tip. Repeat on the other end of the rope. Attach half of the clasp to each of the bead tips.

► Frilly Charms

6 Pick up 40 charlottes and tie a knot to form a ring (figure 6). These beads will become rows 1 and 2.

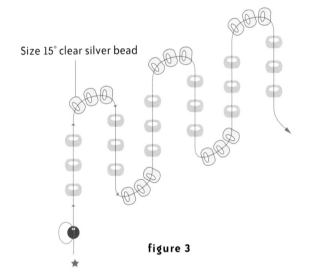

Size 15° clear silver bead

figure 3

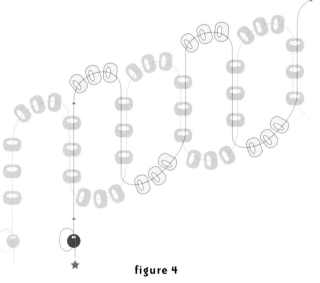

figure 4

96

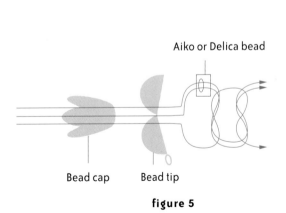

Aiko or Delica bead

Bead cap   Bead tip

figure 5

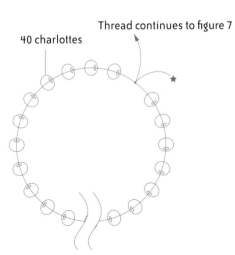

40 charlottes

Thread continues to figure 7

figure 6

7 Using peyote stitch, weave 3 rows with charlottes, 2 rows with Aikos, 1 row with Matsunos, and 2 rows with triangle beads (figure 7). This completes one beaded ring.

8 Repeat steps 6 and 7 to make a second beaded ring, but with one change: The rings should be interlaced, so after you pick up the 40 charlottes, pass your thread through the first ring and only then tie the knot, as shown in figure 8.

9 Make four more rings for a total of six interlaced beaded rings, joining the sixth one to the first and fifth, as shown in figure 9. This completes one frilly charm. Make four more (or any quantity you desire) and run the necklace through them as shown in the illustration.

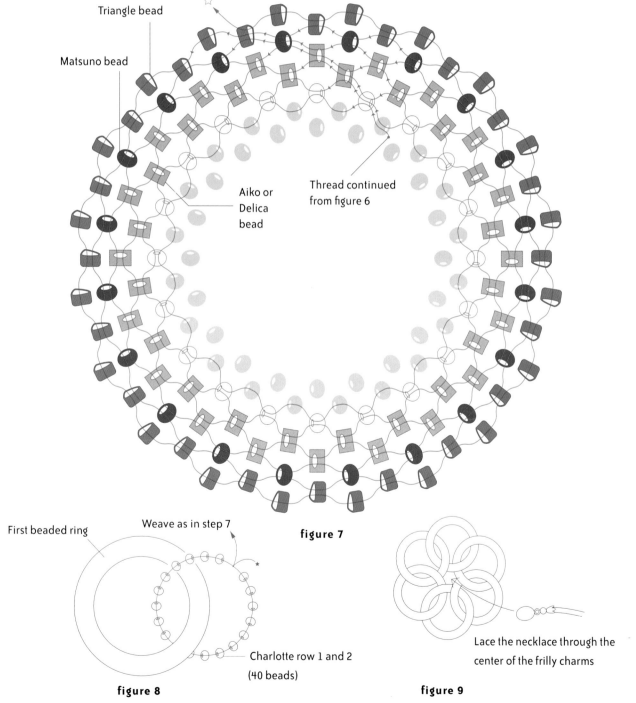

Triangle bead

Matsuno bead

Aiko or Delica bead

Thread continued from figure 6

figure 7

First beaded ring

Weave as in step 7

Charlotte row 1 and 2 (40 beads)

figure 8

Lace the necklace through the center of the frilly charms

figure 9

STONE PAVEMENT

Since I find the distinctive look of Czech beads very appealing,

I use them in this distinctive choker and bracelet set.

▶ Choker

1 Following figures 1 and then 2 (on the next page), string on all beads sequentially from the end. When you string on the petal-shaped beads, alternately have them face up and face down.

2 After stringing all the beads from Row 211 to Row 1, use the hook to stitch tubular crochet with eight chains in one round.

To finish the entire tube, you'll need to attach a total of three new threads. To add them securely to the beadwork, zigzag through the beads to come out from the end of the tube (figure 3, page 101).

CHOKER SUPPLIES

Size 11° beads:

Gilded marbled bronze, 13 g

Marbled white, 2 g

Size 8° gilded marbled bronze beads, 3 g

104 petal-shaped beads

2 size 11° Aiko or Delica beads (any color)

2 gold bead tips

2 gold bead caps

Gold clasp

Crochet hook, size G-6 (4 mm) or H-8 (5 mm)

43¾ yards (40 m) of brown size 8 crochet thread

Size 10 or 12 beading needles

Sharp snips

Glue

STITCH

Tubular Bead Crochet

FINISHED SIZE

15 inches (38 cm) long

This illustration shows just the last 4 rows.
Refer to figure 2 for the rest of the beads to string.

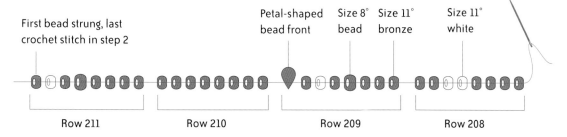

First bead strung, last crochet stitch in step 2

Petal-shaped bead front

Size 8° bead

Size 11° bronze

Size 11° white

Row 211 Row 210 Row 209 Row 208

figure 1

3 At one end of the tube, pass all the threads through a bead cap and a bead tip. Divide the threads into a group of one and a group of two, then add one Aiko or Delica to the group of two (figure 4). Tie a square knot, glue it, and let it dry. Repeat on the other end of the beadwork. Close the bead tips. Finish off the threads then attach the two parts of the clasp, one in each bead tip.

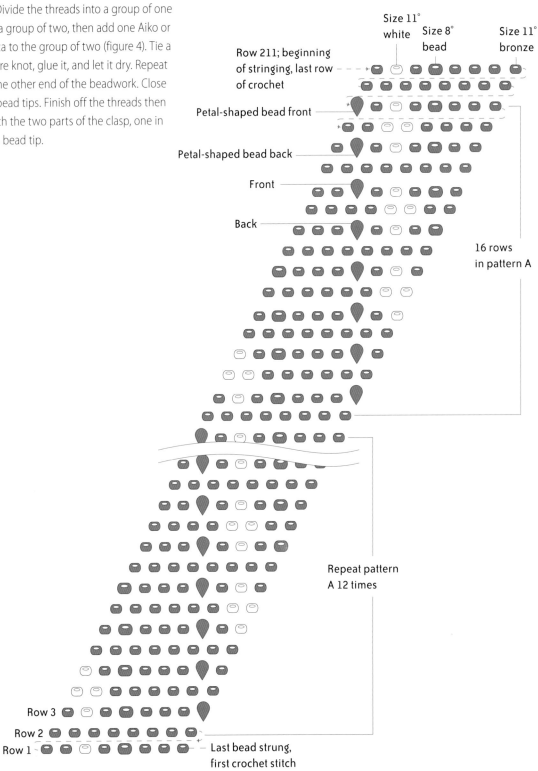

Size 11° white

Size 8° bead

Size 11° bronze

Row 211; beginning of stringing, last row of crochet

Petal-shaped bead front

Petal-shaped bead back

Front

Back

16 rows in pattern A

Repeat pattern A 12 times

Row 3

Row 2

Row 1 — Last bead strung, first crochet stitch

figure 2

100

▶ Bracelet

Follow steps 1 and 2 for the necklace, but make the bracelet half as long. Then attach the ends of the tube to each other, making sure the beads on each side correspond to each other so the tube doesn't twist.

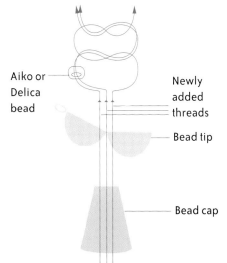

Aiko or Delica bead

Newly added threads

Bead tip

Bead cap

figure 3

figure 4

BRACELET SUPPLIES

Size 11° beads:

Gilded marbled bronze, 7.5 g

Marbled white, 1 g

Size 8° gilded marbled bronze beads, 1.5 g

52 petal-shaped beads

Crochet hook, size G-6 (4 mm) or H-8 (5 mm)

22 yards (20 m) of brown size 8 crochet thread

Size 10 or 12 beading needles

Gray, light gray, and red threads

Sharp snips

FINISHED SIZE

3 inches (7.5 cm) in diameter

CRYSTAL ROSE

In this design, I wrap a large crystal bead with a crocheted tube so that it becomes a flower-shaped form. It's a great way to combine crochet and beadweaving. I taught this as a class at the Bead Art Show in Yokohama in 2008.

SUPPLIES

Size 15° silver beads, 20 g

Silver 11° Delicas, 0.7g

1 crystal-colored rivoli, 27 mm
(Swarovski Elements 3015, Crystal)

35 clear crystal bicones, 3 mm
(Swarovski Elements 5328, Crystal)

2 silver bead caps

Silver clasp

Gray beading thread

43¾ yards (40 m) of gray
size 30 crochet thread

Size 10 or 12 beading needles

Big eye needle

Crochet hook, size G-6 (4 mm) or
H-8 (5 mm)

Sharp snips

STITCHES

Circular Peyote

Netting

Tubular Bead Crochet

FINISHED SIZE

19 inches (48.3 cm) long

70 size
15° beads

figure 1

▶ Bezel

1 Referring to figures 1 and 2 and using circular peyote stitch, weave 4 rows with size 15° beads, 3 rows with Delicas—when you finish the third row of Delicas, put in the rivoli to bezel around it—and then 4 rows with size 15° beads. Keep peyote stitching with size 15° beads while enclosing the rivoli.

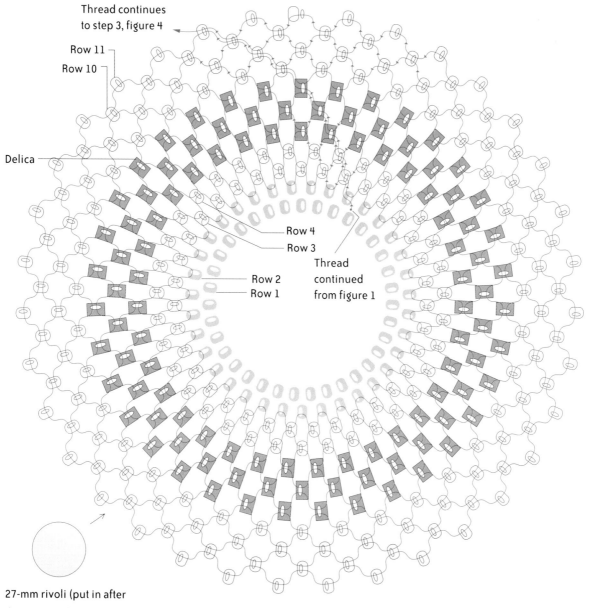

Thread continues
to step 3, figure 4

Row 11
Row 10

Delica

Row 4
Row 3

Thread
continued
from figure 1

Row 2
Row 1

27-mm rivoli (put in after
three rows of Delicas)

figure 2

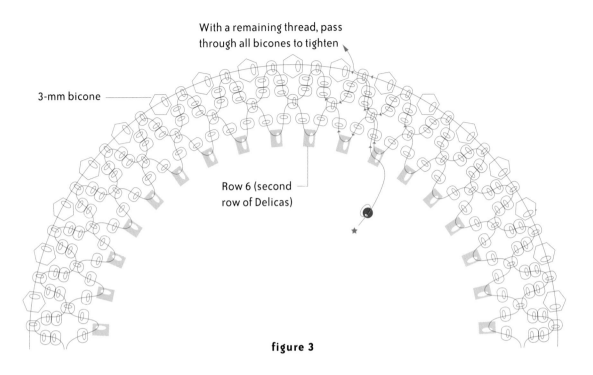

With a remaining thread, pass
through all bicones to tighten

3-mm bicone

Row 6 (second
row of Delicas)

figure 3

2 Add netting embellishments by passing through the beads in row 6 (the second row of Delicas) using 15° beads and bicones, as shown in figure 3. After completing the netting, go through all the bicones two or three times to tighten them.

▶ **Loops**

3 Make two loops on the back side, through which you'll insert the rope later. To make the first loop, pick up 36 size 15° beads on the remaining thread, and pass through the same bead again to make a loop, as shown in figure 4. Pass through the same bead path two or three more times to secure. Weave the working thread over by going through the beads in rows 10 and 11. Make another loop as previously described. Set the piece aside.

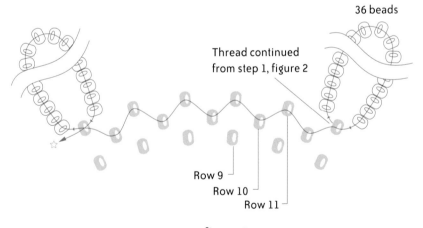

36 beads

Thread continued
from step 1, figure 2

Row 9
Row 10
Row 11

figure 4

▶ Tube

4 String 5,500 size 15° beads—that's most of the 20 grams—onto your crochet thread. Stitch tubular bead crochet with 7 chains in 1 round. Continue crocheting until you have a tube 9 ¾ inches (24.8 cm) long. Intertwine the tube as shown in figure 5, then join both ends as shown in figure 6. Cut the thread. The remaining beads on the cut-off thread will be used in step 6.

5 Attach the bezel to the crocheted tube as described in figure 7.

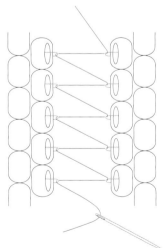

Where both ends butt together, join them as described in figure 6

figure 5

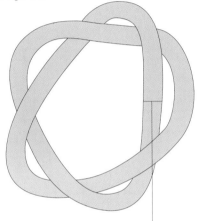

Match up both sides and pass through the beads so that they line up naturally

figure 6

Instead of hanging your beadwork from a rope, you can mount it onto a comb for a stunning hair ornament.

▶ Rope

6 Make a rope of tubular bead crochet—with 7 stitches per round—that's 17¾ inches (45.1 cm) long.

If you run out of crochet thread, thread a new length of crochet thread onto a big eye needle, then transfer over the beads that were originally strung.

Once you reach the desired length, cut off the remaining crochet thread. Cut 3 lengths of beading thread (*not* crochet thread); attach these to one end of the rope by zigzagging them through the tube beads, as shown in the bottom half of figure 8. Also attach 3 lengths of beading thread to the other end of the rope. On each end of the rope, pull all the threads through a bead cap; add 15° beads, half of the clasp, and more 15° beads (figure 8, top). Finish off the threads and run the rope through the loops made in step 3.

Insert the needle from the front. Pick up the thread between the beads of the sixth row (second row of Delicas) and come out from the back. Go through 2 or 3 adjacent size 15° beads of the tube, then come out from the front again. Repeat all around the bezel.

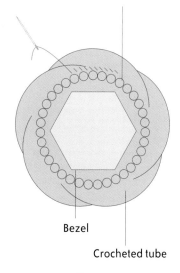

Bezel

Crocheted tube

figure 7

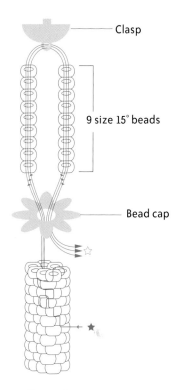

Clasp

9 size 15° beads

Bead cap

figure 8

DAISY

In this double lariat, two ordinary daisy chains are joined together by additional seed beads. With these pretty flower motifs, you can choose calm colors to make a lovely and subtle piece of jewelry.

SUPPLIES

233 green faceted crystal rounds, 4 mm (Swarovski Elements 5000, Crystal Vitrail Medium)

Size 11° metallic bronze beads, 25 g

Size 15° gray beads, 6 g

Gray beading thread

Size 10 or 12 beading needles

Sharp snips

STITCH

Daisy Chain

FINISHED SIZE

41½ inches (105 cm) long

1 Weave a chain with 116 flower motifs in daisy chain stitch (figure 1). Make a second chain in the same way, but with 117 flower motifs. Tie the remaining threads in half-hitch knots and cut the threads off.

2 In this step, you'll use two beading needles and threads. Arrange the chains side by side as shown in figure 2 and pass through the 11° beads on one side of the daisy chains, picking up size 15° beads to connect the two chains together as shown in the illustration. Tie several half-hitch knots in the finished chain, then cut off the threads.

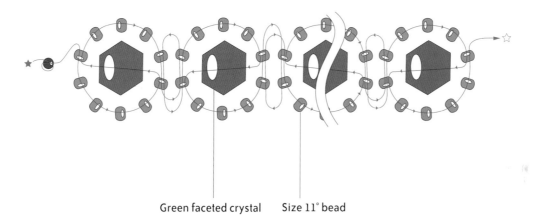

Green faceted crystal   Size 11° bead

figure 1

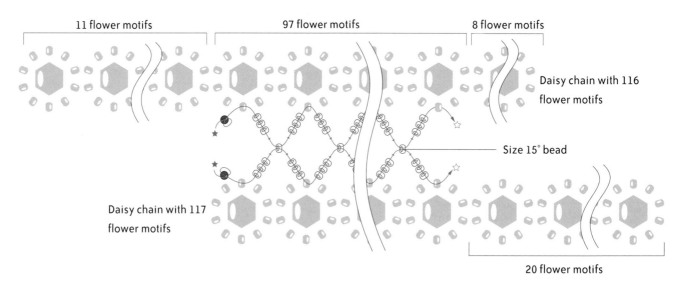

11 flower motifs   97 flower motifs   8 flower motifs

Daisy chain with 116 flower motifs

Size 15° bead

Daisy chain with 117 flower motifs

20 flower motifs

figure 2

SONOKO NECKLACE

In 2005, this design gave me my first opportunity to teach at the Bead&Button Show. The necklace's Asian style makes it very memorable.

SUPPLIES

Silver 13° charlotte beads, 18 g

Silver 11° Aikos, 20 g

Silver 10° three-cut beads, 32 g

Matte white 10° Matsunos, 20 g

2.5-mm blue 10° triangle beads, 30 g

2 French wires, each 2 inches (5.1 cm) long, optional

Silver clasp

Gray beading thread

Size 10 or 12 beading needles

Sharp snips

STITCH

Circular Peyote

FINISHED SIZE

20⅞ inches (53 cm) long

► Circular Motifs

1 Following figure 1, pick up 40 charlottes then tie the thread to form a ring. In the following rows, pick up 20 beads for each round of circular peyote stitch. When you finish weaving row 9, weave in and finish off the threads.

2 Make a new motif, interlocking it (as shown in figure 2) with the motif woven in step 1.

3 Continue making interlocking motifs, combining them in chains to make parts A through E, as explained in figure 3. **Important**: Make two Cs and Ds; they'll serve as the left side of the necklace.

4 Combine parts A through E as follows. As described in figure 3, spiral part B and then stitch it in a well-balanced way onto part A so it fills the center opening. Make sure the attachment thread doesn't show.

5 Make a ring of beadwork as shown in figure 4. Use it to link motifs A11 and E1.

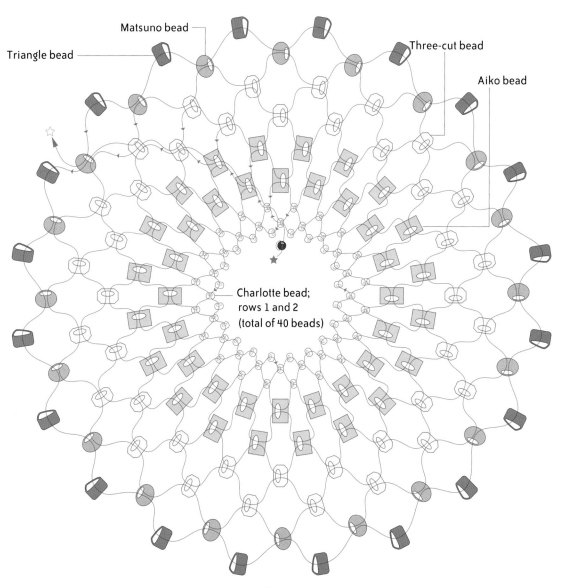

Triangle bead

Matsuno bead

Three-cut bead

Aiko bead

Charlotte bead; rows 1 and 2 (total of 40 beads)

figure 1

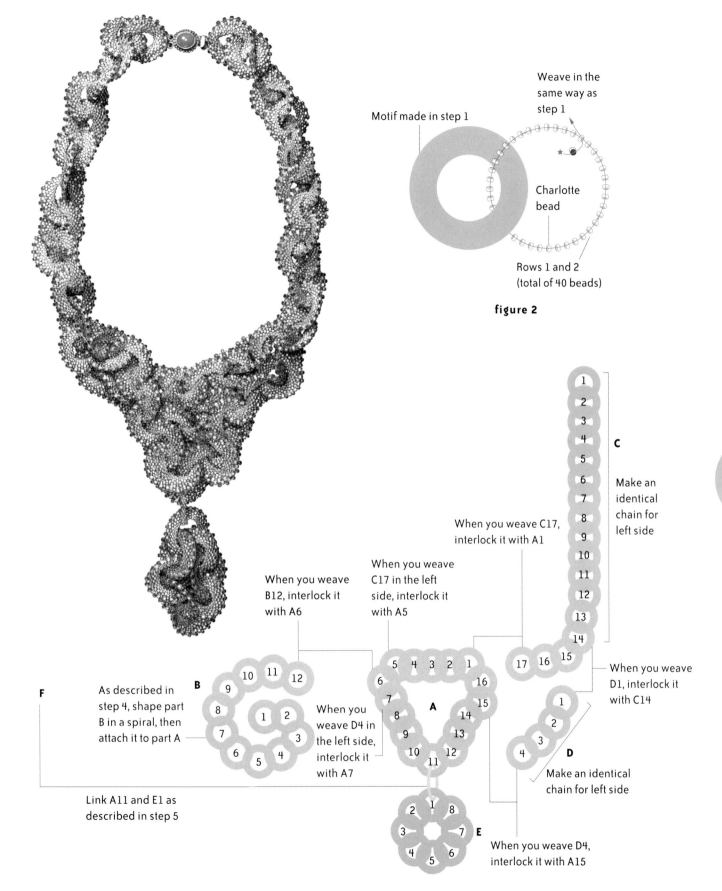

Weave in the
same way as
step 1

Motif made in step 1

Charlotte
bead

Rows 1 and 2
(total of 40 beads)

figure 2

1
2
3
4
5
6
7
8
9
10
11
12
13
14

C

Make an
identical
chain for
left side

When you weave C17,
interlock it with A1

When you weave
C17 in the left
side, interlock it
with A5

When you weave
B12, interlock it
with A6

17   16   15

When you weave
D1, interlock it
with C14

5   4   3   2   1
6   16
7   **A**   15
8   14
9   13
10   12
     11

B
10 11 12
9
8   1   2
7   3
6   5 4

When you
weave D4 in
the left side,
interlock it
with A7

1
2
3
4

D

Make an identical
chain for left side

F

As described in
step 4, shape part
B in a spiral, then
attach it to part A

2   1   8
3   7
4   6
   5

E

When you weave D4,
interlock it with A15

Link A11 and E1 as
described in step 5

figure 3

► Add the Clasp

6 Connect link C1 at each end of the neck-lace to one half of the clasp, referring to figure 5 for the threading pattern. If you use French wires—which are optional—cut them short and put the thread through them without beads.

Charlotte bead;
rows 1 and 2 (total of 40 beads)

Rows 3 and 4
(20 beads in
each row)

figure 4

Clasp

6 charlotte beads (if you use French wires, no beads are necessary)

C1 motif

figure 5

Morning Dew, 2006

33 x 4 x1.8 cm

Crystal chandelier drop, crystal bicones, glass
beads, seed beads; tubular peyote stitch,
bead crochet

PHOTO BY HISAMITSU HAYASHI

Flower Garden, 2010

17 x 10 x 1.8 cm

11° seed beads, magatamas,
lampworked glass bead, clasp;
spiral stitch

PHOTO BY RYUJI NOZUE

RIGHT

Breath of Forest, 2007

21 x 10 x 1.5 cm

Crystal bicones,
seed beads; spiral stitch

PHOTO BY HISAMITSU HAYASHI

BOTTOM

Flash, 2005

28 x 4 x 0.8 cm

2-mm crystal faceted
rounds;
bead crochet

PHOTO BY RYUJI NOZUE

LEFT

Series of Far-Off Memories bag, 2010

18 x 9 x 0.5 cm

Three-cut beads, 15° seed beads,
4-mm crystal faceted rounds, purse frame;
daisy chain stitch

PHOTO BY RYUJI NOZUE

BOTTOM

The Shore, 2010

25 x 5 x 1.5 cm

3-mm crystal bicones, 11° cylinder beads,
Czech petal beads, vintage crystal drop, German clasp;
bead crochet

PHOTO BY RYUJI NOZUE

Mountain Spiral, **2007**

30 x 5 x 1 cm

Toho gilded marble beads and charlotte beads, 3-mm crystal faceted rounds, German clasp; spiral stitch

PHOTO BY RYUJI NOZUE

Gold Sand, **2009**

Necklace, 16 x 10 x 0.5 cm; bracelet, 17 x 1.5 x 0.5 cm

Toho Gold marble beads, charlottes, German magnetic clasp; Red Lake zigzag stitch

PHOTO BY RYUJI NOZUE

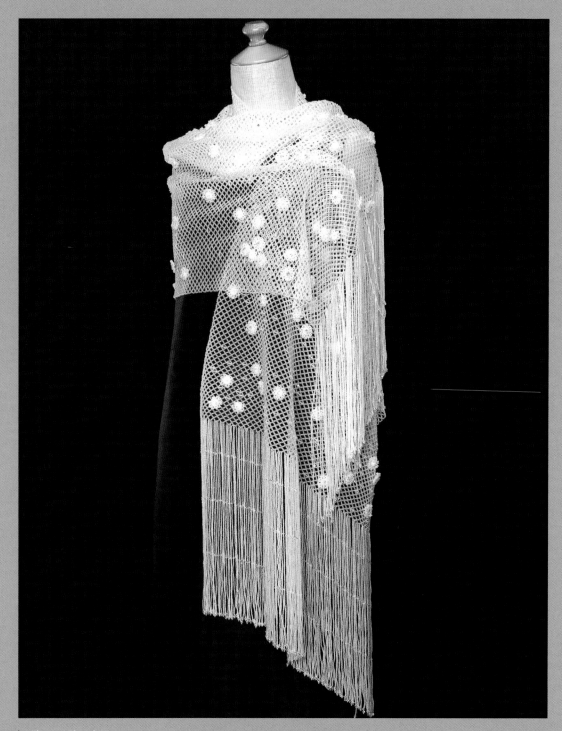

Elegant Shawl, 2009

150 x 50 x 0.8

8° and 11° seed beads, 3- and 4-mm
crystal bicones; netting

PHOTO BY HISAMITSU HAYASHI

ABOVE

Fresh Green, 2005

5.5 x 4.5 x 0.7 cm

Malachite cabochon, crystal
flower-shaped beads, crystal
bicones; tubular peyote stitch

PHOTO BY HISAMITSU HAYASHI

RIGHT

Moonlight, 2004

3 x 2 x 2 cm

Metal beads; tubular peyote stitch

PHOTO BY HISAMITSU HAYASHI

Series of Far-Off Memories bracelet, 2010

19 x 9 x 0.5 cm

Three-cut beads, 15° seed beads, 4-mm crystal faceted rounds, German clasp; daisy chain stitch

PHOTOS BY RYUJI NOZUE

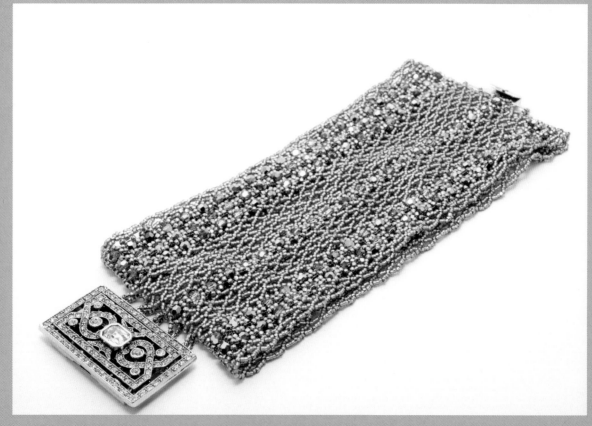

Rippling Waves, 2010

19 x 8 x 1.5 cm

Freshwater pearls, three-cut beads, metal beads, crochet lace thread; bead crochet

PHOTO BY RYUJI NOZUE

Jet Tree, 2009

32 x 5 x 1 cm

4-mm crystal faceted rounds, three-cut beads, 15° seed beads, bead caps, German clasp; daisy chain stitch

PHOTO BY RYUJI NOZUE

Shade of a Tree, 2005

18 x 9 x 0.8 cm

Lampworked glass bead,
crystal bicones; bead crochet

First Snow, 2006

36 x 8 x 0.6 cm

Crystal chatons, 15° cylinder
beads; peyote stitch

PHOTO BY HISAMITSU HAYASHI

LEFT

Lake Side, 2005

16 x 11.5 x 1 cm

Seed beads; double netting

PHOTO BY HISAMITSU HAYASHI

BOTTOM

Peacock, 2009

25 x 4 x 1.6

Cylinder beads, malachite, vintage crystal drop, 2-mm crystal faceted rounds, German clasp; new technique

PHOTO BY RYUJI NOZUE

125

Hazy Moon, 2004

30 x 10 x 2.2 cm

Lampworked glass beads, seed beads, Czech beads

PHOTO BY HISAMITSU HAYASHI

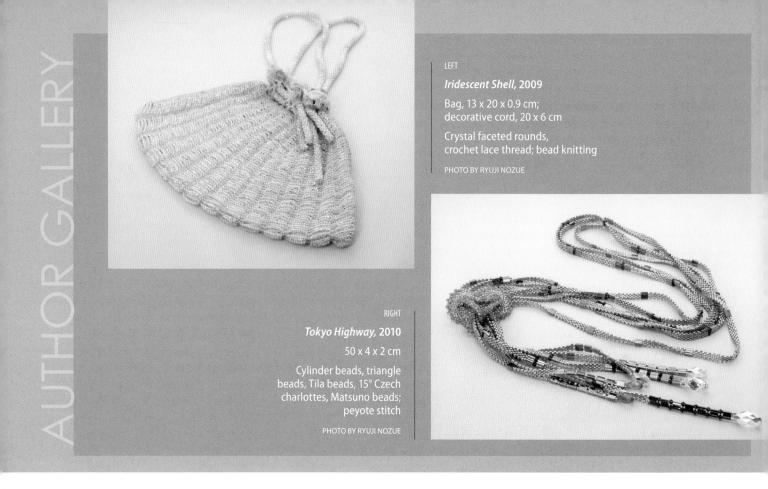

AUTHOR GALLERY

LEFT

Iridescent Shell, 2009

Bag, 13 x 20 x 0.9 cm;
decorative cord, 20 x 6 cm

Crystal faceted rounds,
crochet lace thread; bead knitting

PHOTO BY RYUJI NOZUE

RIGHT

Tokyo Highway, 2010

50 x 4 x 2 cm

Cylinder beads, triangle
beads, Tila beads, 15° Czech
charlottes, Matsuno beads;
peyote stitch

PHOTO BY RYUJI NOZUE

ACKNOWLEDGMENTS

I would like to thank all those in the United States and Japan who faced and overcame the challenges involved in publishing this book. I'm grateful to translator Maki Yamakawa and to Seiko Furuyama, an editor at Wanimagazine, which published this book in its original form in Japan.

I'm fortunate to get some assistance from a couple of bead manufacturers in Japan—Miyuki and Toho—that produce first-class, high-quality product. The Swarovski Company in North America sponsors the lessons I give in the United States, and Swarovski Japan aids my activities in Japan.

Without the help of Diane Fitzgerald, this book would not have become a reality. I've learned a great deal from Diane during our work together, and I look up to her as a teacher. She learned the basics of beadweaving thoroughly in order to spread them to beaders across the world. I greatly admire Diane's attitude of warmly welcoming all those who love beads. I'm proud to have her as my friend.

ADDITIONAL PHOTO CREDITS

PAGE 2

Summer Vacation, 2007

21 x 10 x 1.5 cm

Seed beads, crystal bicones;
spiral stitch

PHOTO BY HISAMITSU HAYASHI

PAGE 11

Four Seasons, 2006

23 x 15 x 2.5 cm

Crystal bicones, seed beads; spiral stitch,
bead crochet

PHOTO BY HISAMITSU HAYASHI

PAGE 127

Cover photo of *Shiny Shiny* reprinted by permission of Ishinsha, © 2011

ABOUT SONOKO NOZUE

Born in Tokyo in 1945. Resides in Japan.

Graduated from the College of Humanities and Science, Nihon University, in 1968, with majors in Japanese and Japanese literature.

Began teaching bead classes in Nagoya in 1995.

President of Bead Salon Sonoko, a group whose activities include organizing workshops taught by the author, producing commissioned beaded pieces for special exhibitions, and participating in events that promote beading in Japan and stimulate interest in this field.

In 2005, became the first foreign instructor at the Bead&Button Show. Since then, has attended this event every year. Her beadwork won the Bead Dreams Finalist in the Seed Beads Wearable category in both 2005 and 2007.

 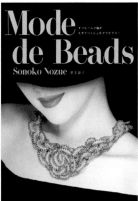 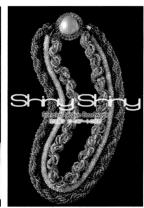

Taught at Bead Art Show Kobe in 2006 and Bead Art Show Yokohama in 2007. In the same year, taught the workshop "CREATE YOUR STYLE with SWAROVSKI ELEMENTS" at the Japan Hobby Show.

Served as a judge for the Bead Grand Prix competition sponsored by *Yomiuri* newspaper and the Japan Art Accessories Association.

Supervised the bead crochet correspondence course taught by the Japan Art Accessories Association.

Authored two beading books in Japanese, *Mode de Beads* (2008) and *Shiny Shiny* (2011).

CREATE YOUR STYLE with SWAROVSKI ELEMENTS Ambassador

Website: http://sonokobeads.jp/

AN ESSENTIAL LIBRARY OF BOOKS FOR BEADERS

Diane Fitzgerald's
SHAPED BEADWORK

dimensional jewelry
with peyote stitch

Diane Fitzgerald

Marcia
DeCoster's
BEADED
OPULENCE

elegant jewelry
projects with
right angle weave

Marcia DeCoster

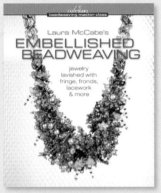

Laura McCabe's
EMBELLISHED
BEADWEAVING

jewelry
lavished with
fringe, fronds,
lacework
& more

Laura McCabe

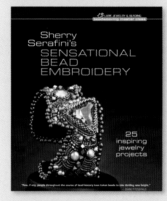

Sherry
Serafini's
SENSATIONAL
BEAD
EMBROIDERY

25
inspiring
jewelry
projects

Sherry Serafini

MAGGIE MEISTER'S
CLASSICAL
ELEGANCE

20
beaded
jewelry
designs

Maggie Meister

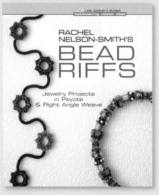

RACHEL
NELSON-SMITH'S
BEAD
RIFFS

Jewelry Projects
in Peyote
& Right Angle Weave

Rachel Nelson-Smith

JAPANESE
BEADWORK
WITH
SONOKO NOZUE

25
Jewelry Designs
from a
Master Artist

Sonoko Nozue

SABINE LIPPERT'S
BEADED
FANTASIES

30 Romantic
Jewelry Projects

Sabine Lippert